Dedication

To Human Rights

This novel is symbolic of a divine torch, which ignites the path of humanity, to enhance the awakening of positivity.

Preface

The United Nations has opened the book, to address crucial issues of mass killings of Tamil civilians, during the final stage of civil war in Sri Lanka. They advocate against military shelling of innocent Tamil civilians. The United Nations probe into alleged war crimes, implemented by the Sri Lankan army, against Tamil civilians. They call for justice to prevail as unlawful mass killings of Tamil civilians, has gained the attention of an international audience. It is time to draw the curtains and expose the substantial issues behind it. Murugathasan Varnakulasingam torched himself in front of the United Nations building in Geneva. His last words jog the memory of an international audience:

"We Tamils, displaced and all over the world, loudly raised our problems and asked for help before the international community in your own language for three decades. But nothing happened... So I decided to sacrifice my life... the flames over my body will be a torch to guide you through the liberation path" (As reported by the Guardian UK).

It is time the war atrocities surface like oil on water. Human rights are imperative, as it introduces humans to the civil and moral codes of conduct, entrenched in our existence. This novel articulates the fundamental need for human rights, through a series of anecdotes. It is time to declare universal peace, inherent in human rights.

CHAPTER 1

The Protest

May 15, 2009, like a swarm of bees a colony was formed. It was a hyperbole of millions of bees who swarmed with success. They were not perceived as a threat but were there to respond to a brutal, bloody, belligerent threat. Like a colony of bees thousands of Sri Lankan Tamils perch themselves on the Gardiner Expressway in Toronto, Canada. Their buzz was imperative, as it was a vital message to the Canadian government to relay a message to the Sri Lankan government. They wanted transparency in the war zone at the end of the bloody civil war in Sri Lanka.

"No More Genocide,

No More Genocide,

No More Genocide,

No More Genocide,

No More Genocide,

No More Genocide!"

These were chants from the vulnerable crowd of Tamils, with overwhelming feelings of anger. Rage set the stage. Midst the heights of the Gardiner Expressway, the bellow of the enraged Tamils echoed through the streets of Toronto. Like a boomerang their cries travelled through the vicinity and back. The magnitude was sufficient to reach the ear of the media and the Canadian government. The velocity of the sound was loud enough to reach the ear of the Sri Lankan government and other human rights organizations. It was a prolonged day and night as the Canadian Tamils cordially sung their bitter song, using the Gardiner Expressway as their stage. Their ultra-high frequency transmitted worldwide. Their sound waves bounced off every television in homes worldwide.

"Today we wave our red flags,

The Sri Lankan genocide drags,

The Sri Lankan civil war conflict,

Brutal pain is what they inflict,

Major Sinhalese and Tamil tension,

Genocide of Tamils in every dimension,

Terror tactics in the north and east,

Tamil civilians met their beast,

The massacre of innocent civilians,

And mass murder by the millions,

The government atrocities began,

Killing of women, children and every man,

Hospitals, homes and schools were shelled,

From their homes they were expelled,

The map of Sri Lanka is a tear drop,

Ironically the tears they had to mop,

A savage civil war left Tamils dead,

To Canada, Tamil refugees fled,

Now we sing a song for peace,

We want to see the war cease,

And the antagonist to blame,

Genocide is not a recreational game,

Destroying a particular ethnic race,

The intent to destroy is a disgrace,

Extermination, a crime against humanity,

Intentional killings out of pure vanity,

Massacre, murder and assassination,

The destruction of the Tamil nation,

The graphic image of the dead,

A dissembled hand, leg, and a head,

Mothers, fathers, sons and daughters,

Vivid images of all the slaughters,

Heinous crimes against humanity,

It's nothing but a case of insanity,

Rape and sexual violence on females,

Persecution on all outspoken males,

Children witnessing graphic bloodshed,

Observing their parents as they bled,

On the Gardiner Expressway we demonstrate,

Sri Lankan Tamils dying at a high rate,

Put an end to the Sri Lankan army shelling,

Our angry voices will continue yelling,

Put an end to the civilian bloodbath,

An end to genocide and a political wrath."

The Tamil demonstrators' heads were filled with a tune of torture, torment, trouble and turpitude. It was a dangerous situation, yet not as dangerous as the war zone in Sri Lanka. Men, women, and children cried out in agony:

No justice no peace,

No justice no peace,

No justice no peace,

No justice no peace,

No justice no peace,

A shuffle broke out between riot police and the demonstrators, as the shielded police exerted physical force. It was the conventional use of power however the police showed empathy. Women in the crowd cried out in anguish.

"He is bleeding. Oh my god he is bleeding."

The blood that trickled down a young male adult's forehead provoked empathy from the female demonstrators. They gave a gut-wrenching, gory, gruesome and growling scream. It was not a matter of life and death. The paradox of the situation was that they were there to empathize with the violent bloodshed in Sri Lanka. The red blood, which gently tricked down his forehead, was a juxtaposition of the bloodshed in the war zones in Sri Lanka. This young man was in a safe place. It boiled down to a case of homophobia. The notion of blood elevated an immediate sense of anxiety, racing heart and rising blood pressure. It was a minor incident on the Gardiner Expressway, which culminated fear. It had no impact on the fate of the brutal bloodshed in Sri Lanka. This sporadic skirmish did not gain the attention of the rest of the chanting crowd.

"No more," part of the crowd chanted.

"Genocide," the other half chorused.

"No more," they elicit a response.

"Genocide," was the reply.

"No more," the chant grew louder.

"Genocide," the answer was brutally clear.

"No more," the crowd was conspicuously clear.

"Genocide," their voices echoed in all dimensions.

On the other end of the spectrum, a journalist engaged in serious conversation with a Canadian Tamil girl. She was a Tamil young adult with a unique Canadian accent. She did not need the Canadian maple leaf flag attached to her backpack. Despite peoples' scepticism about who a Canadian really is, her accent was her birth certificate, which subtly stated that she was Canadian born. She was part and parcel of the "melting pot." Her accent verified her Canadian national identity. Her physical features validated that she embraced the Sri Lankan culture.

"Why are you here?" the journalist was ready to gather information.

"We are demonstrating because of the genocide in Sri Lanka. The war between the majority Sinhalese government and the Tamils began in 1983. It all began when the Sinhalese government wanted Sinhala as the official language. The Sinhalese government passed political laws, which discriminated against Tamils. Most educated Tamils held government jobs... but they lost their jobs. Ethnic tension rose between the majority Sinhalese and minority Tamil citizens of Sri Lanka. In 1983 The Liberation Tamil Tigers of Eelam was formed to retaliate against the Sri Lankan army. On May 15, 2009 the Sri Lankan Government claimed that they defeated the rebels," She narrated.

"What conspired after that?" The journalist took control.

"Well, Tamil civilians lost their lives. This genocide was like an ethnic cleansing. On several occasions the Sri Lankan government forces shelled the areas occupied by Tamils. They placed Tamil civilians in No Fire zones. They continued to bomb these No Fly zones. They were traitors who had no respect for human life. We lost family, friends and relatives in a terrorizing bloodbath," tears filled her eyes.

"Who were killed?" The journalist took lead.

"About 100,000 people died. Thousands of innocent civilians... men, women and children were murdered and massacred. Tamils were killed in hospitals and in the safe zone areas. Each side blamed the other. We are here because of the civilian casualties. No food, no medication, no running water, no medical equipment. The safe zone was a war zone," she was brutally honest.

"Where did this take place?" The journalist was sympathetic.

"Mainly in Vanni," she was emotional.

Their voices drowned by chanting of the crowd.

"Stop that,"

"Genocide,"

"Stop that,"

"Genocide,"

"Stop that,"

"Genocide,"

"When do we want it?"

"Right now!"

"When do we want it?"

"Right now!"

"When do we want it?"

"Right now!"

"Sri Lankan president,"

"War Criminal,"

"Sri Lankan president."

"War Criminal,"

"No justice,"

"No peace,"

"No justice,"

"No peace,"

"No justice,"

"No peace."

"Knock knock,"

"Genocide,"

"Knock knock,"

"Genocide,"

"Knock knock,"

"Genocide,"

Other non Tamil groups joined in for the sake of Human Rights. Like a school of sardines that miraculously washed up on the shore line, the demonstrator's presence was dense and large. Their migration route was dangerous. The current was turbulent. It was a rare phenomena. Their loud and vibrant voices provided Canadians with an insight into their actions.

Those civilians ruthlessly butchered during the war were human beings, inherent with personality traits. They belonged to one ethic group who, deserved the rights of freedom and protection. According to the norms of society, they deserved the rights to live. There is a sector of society who projects all qualities of being an antagonist. They believe that they have the justification to torture and terminate the life of others. The neo cortex of their brain associated with reasoning fails to function. Their cognitive development is stunted. They have no moral and ethical principles to abide by. The Universe generously provides people with abundance of equality, dignity, rights and freedom. The violations of human rights constitute crime. Altruism flourishes in only a few. Human integrity is present in those with altruistic traits. The fundamental right to live in peace is challenged by those who have no virtue to recognise human rights. Each person recognizes their inner strength and independence. However, like a patch work quilt humanity relies on each other for survival. A patch work quilt relies on each other to emerge as a whole. Each patch boasts a different color, shape and texture. It has an impact when it is recognised as a whole. As a whole it projects as a symbol of warmth and comfort. This analogy is a progressive measure to declare "man" as one nation of warmth and comfort.

"Human Rights"

"Human Rights"

"Human Rights"

"Human Rights"

"Human Rights"

"Human Rights"

"Human Rights"

The crowd of Tamil protesters delved deep down into the Canadian Charter of Rights, as they saw it as a catalyst to promote peace. Most of them fled Sri Lanka as refugees, fleeing from evil war. Their home became a slaughter house, with a prominent smell of blood. It was a bitter sweet moment for them. It was bitter to leave behind family and friends, yet sweet to enter a country that met their human needs. Like animals in a slaughter house they witnessed family members slit, shot and left to bleed. In utter disrespect they were thrown into mass graves like contaminated waste. The gruesome sight was a lingering image in their minds. It evoked all their senses. The smell of human remains, with emphasis on remains, it remains in their olfactory nerve. The grime feeling of tasting ones' own blood piles up in their memories, like data saved in a computer. It was a sense of gestation. The touch of open wounds governed their days in the war zone. It was a severe sense of somatosensation. The five senses became the antagonist. The sense of hunger and thirst haunted them. The mind played games on them.

These refugees escaped from the horrors of war. However, they struggle to escape from a tormented mind. Their minds become a war zone, with cluttered thoughts and inner dialogue. The firing rates of negative thought pattern filled the mind. Their mind became their chariot. The five senses are the five white horses that manoeuvres the chariot as orchestrated,

"Free our people"

"Genocide"

"Free our people"

"Genocide"

"Free our people"

"Genocide"

"Free our people"

"Genocide"

"Free our people"

"Genocide"

The words bounced from one group to the next, like a game of volleyball. Their words became a grounding ball, thrown from one court to another. One team rallied by serving words like a ball. The other served back. It echoed throughout the world. The sentiments were felt in Europe.

Woman with children in strollers were nestled in the crowd. The vulnerable children were part of the chaos. They were symbols of innocence. They were there for the fundamental rights for all children. The children in conflict zone faced the barbaric, ruthless and insane atrocities of the antagonist. Children experienced mutilation, massacre, murder, madness and sexual abuse, in the Sri Lankan war zone. The barbaric soldiers had no qualms in exploiting children. The children in the demonstration were young, yet under parental protection. The children in the war zones had to fend for themselves. They were naive and easily manipulated. The anguish of losing their parents and their psychological trauma has a negative impact on their development. The brutal repercussions follow them into their future. Humiliating hostilities followed them around like a shadow.

On the Canadian Gardiner Expressway, two toddlers sat side by side saddled in strollers. Their lives were not a daunting challenge, as those children in the war zone. They were challenged by boredom and out of blissful ignorance, entertained themselves.

"No more war"

"Dinosaurs"

"No more war"

"Dinosaurs"

"No more war"

"Dinosaurs"

"No more war"

"Dinosaurs"

Their conceptual obsession with dinosaurs occupied their minds. That's the norm of every child in today's society. The pendulum swings from children in a protected society, to those Tamil children in the war zone. Their intense interest included images of a real bona fide human soldiers. Human soldiers were their paraphernalia. With innocent minds, the war zone children unlocked the essential history of soldiers in war. The dinosaur phase would never be part of their play routine. Essential entertainment evoking evolution and extinction, was not part of their childhood. The catastrophic lives of dinosaurs and their extinction, will continue to grow in the imagination of children today. As a juxtaposition, the atrocities of real soldiers are embedded and etched in the minds of those children in the bloodied war zone.

Phonetically, the toddlers at the demonstration were not challenged by the names of their favourite dinosaurs,

"Brontosaurus"

"Tyrannosaurus"

"Mapusaurus"

"Ankylosaurus"

"Allosaurus"

"No more dinosaurs"

"No more dinosaurs"

"No more dinosaurs"

"No more dinosaurs"

"No more dinosaurs"

They chanted with high pitched voices. Their minds were on the catastrophic extinction of dinosaurs. The adult demonstrators sang a different tune. Their focus was on the catastrophic extinction of Tamil civilians in the Sri Lanka. Their chants vibrated their world. The murmuring of voices and the beating of the Tamil drums bombarded their stage.

A foreigner perched up on one of the railings with a professional camera as his weapon, gained knowledge from one of the eager demonstrators.

"Hello dear, can you expand on your motivation to demonstrate today," he vocalized.

"Yes," an eager male boasted in his Canadian accent.

"We are here because of the genocide against Tamils, by the Sri Lankan government. They want to wipe out the Tamil nationals by killing thousands. They inflicted mental and physical pain on men, woman, and children. The aim is to destroy a whole Tamil race. They prevented Tamil women from baring more children. This is human rights violation. We cannot stand by and watch family, friends, relatives and our community be destroyed. The Sinhalese mob destroyed Tamil business in Colombo. The Sinhalese mob attacked Tamil protesters protesting against Sinhala as an official language. False rumours are being spread about Tamil led atrocities. Tamils were attacked on trains in Jaffna, Colombo and Hill Country. Tamils were massacred. Tamil political and civil leaders were assassinated. Women and children were raped. They had no food, basic needs and medicine. The government soldiers forced Tamils out of their homes by shelling them. Journalist and aid could not reach them. From 2006 to 2009, there was bloodshed. Tamils sought refuge in Vaharai and Tamil Nadu. Are you a journalist, sir?" his speech came to an abrupt end.

"No, I am a Canadian who is interested in learning about your demonstration. It saddens me, eh! We need human rights, no political injustices. So go on..." he retorted.

"Ok, in 2009 Tamils were sent to the No Fire Zone. The government soldiers fired on three No Fire Zones. Even the United Nations station was shelled. Government shelling killed thousands of Tamils. People on the beach who tried to escape were shelled too. The Tamils in the Vanni region were killed. The Tamils are aware of the government "white van" that picked up Tamil journalist and leaders. They were tortured and killed. Women and children were mutilated. This is ethnic Tamil cleansing. Several makeshift hospitals were shelled by the government. After the Sinhala Only Act of 1970 university admissions favoured only Sinhalese students. It was difficult for Tamil students to enter university. Discrimination against Tamils! Tamil intellectuals were pushed out of the work force. Most of the shelling was in the North East parts of Sri Lanka. The government prevented goods, food, medical supply and humanitarian aid from entering the region. The Sinhalese government reported that there were 75,000 Tamils in the No Fire Zone in April 2009. The truth is there were 300,000 or more Tamil civilians in the No Fire Zone. Tamil lands were confiscated. The Sinhala Buddhist culture rampaged the Tamil areas. Tamil street signs were changed to Sinhalese. Doctors sterilized and performed abortions on Tamil women, without their consent," the young Tamil man was filled with emotions, as he choked up tears.

"I am so sorry, eh! Ethnic cleansing. It reminds me of the Genocide in Rwanda. The Hutu majority government slaughtered masses of Tutsi people. Then the persecution of the Hazora people in Afghanistan. The Pastuns occupied their land. Cruel, just so cruel! Go ahead brother, you have a story to narrate," he validated being an attentive listener.

"We are asking our Canadian government to bring about a political solution. This is a crime against humanity... a genocide. We want to see peace and justice for the Tamil people in Sri Lanka. Measures have to be taken to restore order. The Liberation Tigers of Tamil Eelam better known as the LTTE were given the mandate by the Tamils to retaliate against the government. This fuelled the fire. They wanted self government in the Northeast. The hostilities have to end.

That is imperative. Negotiations, and hostilities have to end. We want to see long lasting peace. Bloody battle, turmoil, suicide, assassination, army raids, murder, rape, sexual slavery, hostage taking, arson, shelling and genocide, has to end," he was well versed on the Sri Lankan genocide.

"That's a lot to digest, eh! Nevertheless, I will join in the chants and marches," he revealed empathy.

"No more"

"Genocide"

"No more"

"Genocide"

"No more"

"Genocide"

"No more"

"Genocide"

The man with the camera envisioned such a perplexed bombardment. He manoeuvred himself into the crowd and took a political stand. There was no reason for apathy, in a course that deserved human rights. He analysed the situation from a psychological, philosophical and feminist lens. It taught him that his logical thoughts could not be suppressed.

Darkness set in as the radiant sun began to set. Darkness brought in a gloomy atmosphere. It emanated a dark dreamy dangerous night. It cancelled the faces of those in the crowd. The Gardiner Expressway was engulfed by the darkness of the night. This darkness was felt by Tamils in Ottawa too. The darkness blanketed the sky. The demonstrators hurdled together, under the cover of blackness. They had to restore their vision in the blackness of the dark night. Not even the children were prone to fear on that dark night. They embraced the dark. They were not afraid of the dark night. However, they were afraid of the dark side of man. Part of humanity projects a dark side, which victimizes other humans. That deviant side of man is the dark side. When politicians, soldiers and people prey upon the innocent civilians, that darkness is tormenting. The impulse to engage in predatory behaviour to kill groups of people is dark. The victimizations of innocent Tamil civilians in Sri Lanka is a symbol of darkness. The predator who kills, shells, massacres, murders, assassinates is a deviant, with a dark side.

Psychopathic and deviant behaviour is present in human condition, relating to their dark side. Predatory behaviour in human beings has a purpose and is motivated by racism and other social factors. Humans portray dark characteristics. Bullying, terrorism, rape, violence, religious fanatics all exhibit the dark side of human beings, which leads to the victimization of others. Their world revolves around perceptual distortions. When a political sector, engages in such malicious and vicious behaviour it is definitely a psychopathological behaviour.

Jealousy related to seeing a person or group of people climbing the social ladder in difficult fields, is another factor that motivates such vicious acts of destruction. A sector of human beings has an obsessive preoccupation to destroy others through violence. It is as if they have a full time job to destroy others. This ritualistic killing becomes a fixation. The egotistical power of a governing body is evident when they seek gratification in destroying a part of their nationals. No man should exhibit the right to torture another for monetary gain and power. This bizarre behaviour has deep seated roots in psychopathological development. The plight of inflicting pain on others is man's distorted perception of reality. Premeditated mass killings are bizarre and insane. It manifests the dark side of humanity. The endeavour of any human to destroy another is a serious act of deviant behaviour. The extensive, elaborate, evil, egotistical endeavours, to commit violence against another, lacks logic and purpose in life. These atrocious acts of violence portrays the dark side of human beings.

It is also profoundly disturbing when people engage in rhetoric, associated with the condemnation of others. Bullying, name calling, violent vernacular and aggressive articulation promotes evil in our society. From an early age at school, teachers promote a peaceful climate by asking children to refrain from such action or rhetoric. However, when grown adults and politicians engage in such violent rhetoric, it sways the crowd into believing that the mode of behaviour is entertaining. Like an advertisement, it appeals to the logos, ethos and pathos of society. This type of rhetoric instigates violence in children and adults. Ironically, it also instigates other politicians to speak with the same negative rhetoric. It is the case of "monkey see, monkey do". It becomes a relay. When another group of people are offended by the fork tongue, they retaliate with physical violence. The layman joins radical groups, which leads to mass assassinations and genocide. Ignorance breeds ignorance.

History unfolds like a book. Each chapter in life dismantles a new issue. A peaceful demonstration reveals passion, promise, peace and unity. It is the triumph over all evil. The dark was illuminated by the lighting of candles. It symbolized the spirit of peace and truth. The divine light illuminated the Gardiner Expressway in Toronto, Canada. Likewise, Tamils in Switzerland and Australia supported the cause. The powerful, positive, peaceful and spiritual energy was present. The energy of the lit candle mingled with the crowd, illuminating their peaceful protest. As each candle was lit the chants of the crowd transposed into a deep meditative process. It permeated an atmosphere of peace and sustained unity of the crowd. The lit candle reignited a sense of spiritual freedom. The candle was a symbol of peace from the universe. It was affirmations that the gateway to freedom and peace, was in the path of the demonstrators.

"What a peaceful protest," a demonstrator acknowledged.

"An aspect of Satyagraha," another held firmly.

"Gandhi's principle of nonviolence lives in us," the girl rendered.

"Yes, the truth. The Tamil community in Canada supports the theory of satyagraha. We are a non violent community. Mohandas Karamchand Gandhi... Mahatma Gandhi was a great Indian leader who put his life on the line to bring about peaceful change in South Africa: he believed that we should not change the opinion of another by force. He believed in passive change. Honesty and the truth will help us in this demonstration. We cannot solve a problem by fighting. We can solve a problem through peaceful demonstration as we are doing now. The faith in our God will pull us through. Tamil also protested in the UK," he gave a sermon.

"Well said sir, Mahatma Gandhi's discipline still lives in us today. We all are here demonstrating because we are in search of the truth. This is a mass demonstration, yet we follow the rules of Satyagraha. For sure...," she coined in her thoughts.

"Our children are present here today to express the nature of passive resistance. We are a perfect role model to these children born under a democratic government. God bless their souls. They will learn from us how to deal with struggles through non violent methods. They will learn how to combat problems," he spoke with passion.

"True! Thank you..." she was unable to complete her sentence as the chant resumed.

"Stop the genocide"

"Free our people"

"Stop the genocide"

"Free our people"

"Stop the genocide"

"Free our people"

"Stop the genocide"

"Free our people"

Their chants resembled a mantra. It was a sincere, soulful, sacred and spiritual utterance. It sounded like a spiritual melody, entrenched in the philosophy of Hinduism and other religious sectors. Ironically, the loud chanting instilled a profound sense of spiritual calmness, in the demonstrators. Peace confronted them with satisfaction. In the dark of the night, the chanting elevated their consciousness to a new level.

Years passed by like a freight train. People obtained information through the grapevine. A new conversation germinated, as a conversation grew. Like the process of germination, the conversation sprouted, expanding from a seed into a greater existence. The conversation spread throughout the crowd, like wild mustard seeds. The conversation did not need sunlight to germinate. Like weeds in a garden it spread out of control.

"Did you hear of Dr. Varatharajah?" a male voice was genuinely concerned.

"Yes, he was one of the five doctors who treated patients in the NO FIRE ZONE" a female showed interest.

"He put his life on the line to save war casualties and reported incidents to the world. He sacrificed his family life to tend to those who were seriously hurt," there was hurt in his voice.

"These doctors are the only witnesses to slaughter, assassinations and murder of the Tamil civilians. The civilians killed in a period between January 2009 to May were about 8,000," another joined into the conversation.

"No, it was about 21,000. Dr. Varatharajah admitted that he was forced to lie, under the pressure of the Sri Lankan government. Because these doctors had key evidence, they were arrested by the government. Under duress they were forced in lie to the public. Their lives were at stake. How humiliating it must have been for the doctors? They had to rehearse that only a few civilians were shelled. That's what Dr. Varatharajah told the United Nations. The government also asked the Red Cross to leave the "no fire zone." The Tamils were given no medication and food," tears streamed down his face with empathy.

"So sorry uncle, that was ethnic cleansing. They want to eliminate all Tamil Civilians... the government that is. That is so insane," she cried.

"Also the army shelled the hospital in the No Fire Zone... I mean the Sri Lankan army. Patients were killed. Even the pediatric ward was shelled. The government blamed the Liberation Tigers of Tamil Eelam, LTTE for the shelling..." he was interrupted.

"Which hospital?" another was curious.

"Pathukkudiyiruppu hospital, but Dr. Varatharajah Thurairajah was in the Mullaittivu district, in the north. Dr. Varatharajah said that five shells hit the hospital on Sunday night. Five women died and many were wounded too. They shelled the hospital at different times too," he was chatty.

"How do they know who fired?" she was in disbelief.

"Dr. Varatharajah confirmed that all the shelling came from the side where the army took position. They had about 600 wounded. They did not care that the hospital was shelled. They visited the hospital to be treated. This made the hospital so crowded. Can you imagine a hospital supposed to be a safe place and it was shelled? Humans killing humans! That's so disgusting," his voice cracked with emotions.

"Where are human rights? How can such barbaric acts happen? The Tamil people wanted an independent Tamil state in the northern and eastern parts, named Tamil Eelam. That's when all the conflict began. Now the government army boasts that that they defeated the Tamil Tigers. That's why the war ended. OK, then why do they continue to attack innocent Tamil civilians? That's genocide...right? That is abuse of human rights. Seriously! This is so sad!" she voiced her opinion.

The major goal of the demonstrators was to initiate peace in Sri Lanka. They wanted the Sri Lankan government to be transparent. They wanted to sustain stability for their family, friends and relatives trapped in the war zone. The demonstrators were not affiliated to any political group. They constituted a group; of demonstrators who collaborated to influence the Canadian government, to save humanity in Sri Lanka. They were activists who shared a common political goal, which was peace. They advocated that the Canadian government should negotiate to stop inhumane crimes against Tamils in Sri Lanka.

The Canadian Government reacted by not attending the Commonwealth summit, which was held in Colombo, Sri Lanka. The Canadian Government adhered to all principles of Human Rights. They did not support the genocide and minority harassment in Sri Lanka

"It is clear that the Sri Lankan government has failed to uphold the Commonwealth's core values, which are cherished by Canadians," the Canadian Government reported to the news media.

The Canadian government held onto its huge, massive bullhorn. It had the loudest built in amplifier and microphone to announce to the world that Canadians believe in Human Rights.

CHAPTER 2

No Fire Zone

Years later, I found out about the Tamil protests worldwide. Ironically, I was at war with myself as well. This internal battle was agonizing. I felt an internal genocide. My entire body split in two parts, which was distressing. There was a civil war inside my head. It was a large case of analysis paralysis. My mind was like a cerebral hurricane. My id and ego were in conflict with each other. Overwhelming thoughts spun around like a gush of wind, causing havoc in my mind. Medical school did not prepare me for such inner turmoil. Neither did it prepare me for a war zone.

"Dr.Varatharajah... please help me!" his voice was a turbulence.

"Help, help... Dr V, help me," I faced fear and failure.

"Dr V.T she is dying," humiliation and guilt took control.

"Yes...yes... yesss!" were the only words I knew.

I walked around the makeshift hospital like a zombie. Nasty negative nagging thoughts filled my mind. I tried to adhere to my sincere principles, taught to me in medical school. However, I had to procrastinate before treating patients. My voice took a leave of absence. I looked at death in its face. Death rode around the makeshift hospital in his black carriage. Death alienated us from our God and Deities. Some patients wrestled with death. Other patients gave in to Death's charming personality. He caused havoc in out makeshift hospital. It was pandemonium as each patient gave in to death, as if they had the potential to live in paradise, in their new spiritual realm. Death provided them with an optimistic vision. I was hopeless. I could not provide them with any helpful prediction. I could not provide them with any medication, operating tools, food or a hospital bed. The frustration of not receiving any medical supplies from the Sri Lankan government frustrated me. I felt self-tormented. Death became my enemy. He revealed his strength to me. I was taught to save lives as a doctor. Death proved to me that he was stronger, which placed me in a hurtful threshold. As each patient left me, guilt followed me around. Death tarnished my reputation.

"Awwww..pain..pain," she cried as blood oozed out.

"Safe, doctor safe… we are?" another patient cried.

"Yes, we are in a no fire zone," I assured them.

The hospital was in shambles. It was a makeshift hospital in an old broken down ruin. A building that was broken down by shelling and air strikes, became a safe haven for Tamil civilians, who were brutally wounded. There was a triage yet no walls and doors. There were make shift tents made from sheets of tarp. It was erected by pieces of tree branches. It was a safety shelter yet patients were still exposed to the elements of wind, rain and extreme heat. Patients slept on the ground on the soft sand. The soft sand was like a sand dune. It was a gruelling task walking on the sand. It was as if it was God's makeshift grave. When the hospital was shelled, the soft, sand sinkholes swallowed the dead. God excavated the land and buried his poor, pinning people. Their sand encrusted bodies sunk into the solid graves. The gaping crater formed their graves, with no erected tombstones. The hospital was a complicated, chaotic, cannibalize, catastrophic and condemned place for the chronically ill.

"Amma, amma, amma, amma," a toddler cried overwrought with emotions.

"Ok... okay," other frenzied patients responded.

"Amma, amma, amma, amma," she screamed at the top of her lungs.

"Ok... okay," other patients barely had strength.

"Amma... amma... amma," mucous streamed down her face as she hysterically threw her hands in the air.

I stared at her in despair. This was a perplexed persecution for me. I wondered about human dignity. From the depth of my fragile soul I cried. My emotions took control of me. The magnitude of her cries struck me like a dagger through my heart. In her face, I saw my own child. My own baby's face flashed up in front of me, like a bright orb. I left home months ago. My baby was three months old. Since then I did not see my wife and baby. My accomplished purpose in life was to take care of patients, in the war zone. I was a government doctor and a chief doctor in charge of the patients in the war zone. I had to provide grace to my humble patients. I was eternally separated from my own family, by the grace of God. I was ostracized by the magnitude of the toddlers screams. That was my penalty of death. In her voice, I heard the voice of my own child.

"Appa save me... Appa come back... save me... please save me appa... appa... appa... do not go away...

come back please." The torture of hearing my own child's voice in this little girl, suffocated me.

"Okay... ok... ok... okay!" I murmured as if comforting my own soul.

Empathy followed me around like a shadow. I was given the responsibility to provide my wounded patients with eternal life. It was a heart wrenching situation, as I wiped away my tears. Pain dwelled in my heart. I chose to live by strength, hope and sincerity. I shook the head of courage. It was a time of trial and tribulation. I did not fail or forsake my patients.

"Doctor... doctor, pain," a woman cried as she drove in and out of consciousness.

"I will give you a drip," I consoled her.

"Doctor, doctor pain," she chanted like a mantra.

I prepared an IV bag for her, with saline fluids, to deliver medication to her intravenously. However, we were running out of saline fluids and the ubiquitous plastic bags. I could not hang the bag three feet above the patient's heart because the makeshift hospital did not have any IV poles. Spontaneously, I had to improvise and hang the IV on the branch of a tree. The government did not send us enough medication and medical tools to perform operations, and treat patients wounded by bombs.

"Doctor I'm thirsty," a patient cried.

"Doctor water," it became a chorus.

"We have no water," I whispered with guilt, because I could not satisfy my patients basic biological drive.

"Please doctor water please," I could not provide them with a balanced internal environment.

"Sorry the government did not send us water," I could not help them maintain their homeostasis.

"Doctor I'm hungry," another looked at me with scrutiny.

"Sorry we have no more food left," their central nervous system could not fathom life without food.

"No more food left," they experienced cellular dehydration.

"No more food left," they chorused.

I realized that the last meal that I had was at 11pm the night before. Our physiological needs were not met. I empathized with them because I was hungry and thirsty too. Our needs to be nourished were denied. The basic human needs were not satisfied. We were depleted of our physiological needs. That deprivation took a toll on our mental health. The Sri Lankan government deprived us of food in the No Fire Zone. To focus exclusively on food and to be denied of food drives a person to psychological torture.

Hunger and thirst were demons that confronted us. They were malevolent creatures who hung above us like a grey cloud. Hunger and thirst were harmful spiritual entities that took possession over our brains. Hunger and thirst did not negotiate with us. Evil prevailed over good. Hunger and thirst enlightened us about death. Our fundamental human needs could not be met. The manifestation of food did not come with magic. This was our purging punishment, inflicted by another human being. The Sri Lankan government presented themselves as hate mongers. They imperatively introduced us to the term starvation. It was a genuine case of eliminating majority of the Tamil civilians. Starvation became an effective weapon to eliminate the doctors who saw too much of evil. It was a torment against humanity. I wondered about the outside world and the United Nations. I wondered if God promoted human rights.

I had to postpone my thoughts of hunger and thirst, like postponing a meeting. At the top of my agenda was patient care.

"Doctor come quick," It was a silent whisper.

"Doctor my mouth is tingling," another showed immediacy.

"Help, help, help," he shook as if it was convulsions.

"I am sweating Doctor," she cried, with a fatigue look.

"I cannot see," another had visual disturbances.

"Doctor, my son is unconscious," he tugged onto my leg.

Immediately, I diagnosed all the symptoms as hypoglycaemia. Most of my patient's sugar levels dropped like a time bomb. I could not treat them for hypoglycaemia. It was not possible to higher their blood sugar levels. We did not have food, sweet drinks, water and medications. A few of them went into seizures. Postprandial hypoglycaemia set in with patients who had surgery. I watched others die instantly. The building was total nightmare guttered by blood. The administration, medical theatre and intensive care unit, were matter of spaces. The destruction of the hospital was a nightmare, fuelling more pain and suffering. Patients slept on tarps on the floor. The circumstances were unhygienic. It was an endangered, extreme and notorious setting, open to aerial assaults.

Patients slept side by side, like sardines that washed up one shore. There were no beds. Wounded men, women and children slept side by side on the floor, in an open area. We had a hospital with imaginary walls. Some casualties slept on the dirt floor outside the old school ruin, which became a makeshift hospital.

It evoked all sense of sight. It became hell on earth. The poignant sight of blood on the floor was prominent. Around the perimeter of the old ruin, big black flies clustered together on rotting human carcasses. They clustered around the makeshift lavatory. There was an army of flies, that challenged patients. The flies spotted bodies like poppy seeds on a bagel. Apart from the challenge of the Sri Lankan army, the wounded were challenged by an army of flies. Those flies laid their larvae in the wounds of patients, which became maggots.

The flies rooted themselves deep into the skin of patients, as if they had invaded their bodies.

The hospital was bombarded by shells. It approached at high speed from the government artillery strikes. The government besieged areas occupied by the LTTE army, firing intensified. We knew that the bombardment was fired from the side of the government, because of the sound and side it originated from. During the pause, the hospital was attacked. We were able to monitor the angle and sound of the shellfire. The artillery shelling was controlled by the government army, targeting the makeshift hospital in the No Fire Zone.

"How can we evacuate the wounded," another doctor was solemn.

"We have no humanitarian aid," I was exhausted.

"The government siege on food, water and medication," the other doctor stammered.

"Civilians are malnourished and dying," the level of urgency was in my voice.

"We cannot venture outside the No Fire Zone, that is so dangerous. There are snipers all around," I was bound to monitor my patients.

"We have to monitor the humanitarian condition. The government siege seems to be tightening. We are surrounded by snipers, landmines, and shelling. We are under siege," the other doctor was concerned about the critically wounded civilians.

Hundreds of thousands of wounded civilians were stranded in the north east, No Fire Zone. The armed conflict took a heavy toll on Tamil civilians. There was an estimate of about 350,000 wounded by shelling.

"Doctor, I'm hungry," a heavily pregnant women cried.

"We ran out of food," I was humble.

"Doctor, I want to die," she cried.

"No," my voice took a leave of absence.

"If I die, I will get lots of food in Heaven," she looked for a logical explanation.

Starvation was a galvanizing factor, which impacted my patients. I experienced a chronic form of malnutrition. Like a vehicle that runs out of gasoline, my body was out off food. Like a bankrupted individual searching for money, my body went into a metabolic mode in search of food.

The heavily pregnant woman in front of me, needed to metabolize nutrients for her and her baby. I stared at her with a poker face. I could not reveal my tension and anxiety. The sight in front of me was an imagery from a horror movie. My emotions ran high. She was close to due date. Her wounds were a fundamental threat to her unborn baby. She was hit by shrapnel, from a shell. She was hurt by flying shrapnel from a mortar shell. The highly dangerous explosive was lodged by the Sri Lankan army. The projectiles were expelled and travelled along the trajectory aimed at the Tamil homes, camps and hospital. The shell velocity targeted the Tamil civilians. Her belly was ruptured by the shrapnel, with highlighted force. It was lethal to both the mother and the baby.

The bomb shell exploded close to her. Her injury was life changing and death defying. The impact of the shrapnel marred her flesh and exposed a gaping hole, in her belly. The projectiles penetrated her body. I could not anticipate treatment or surgery. The tissue disruption was of a huge proportion. Like a hatchling, the baby's hand propelled through the gaping wound. With a hard jab, the baby's arm exited the mother's womb. The baby's hand protruded out of the wound from the fingertip up to the elbow. With involuntary contractions, the hand manoeuvred itself through the muscular walls and burst into the outside world.

The placenta was an oxygen and nutrient provider. Like a snake slithering, it made its way through the uterus and out the gaping wound.

It was as if the baby preformed its own Caesarean section. It conducted its own obstructed labour. The baby created its own incision through the wound on the mother's belly. It was a rare phenomenon. Bonding attachment was visible. The baby explored the mother's tummy by touching her skin, as a bonding motion. Sadly, it was only one arm visible, through the gaping wound.

The notion of innocence reflects on the purity of every child that enters the world. Each child enters the world with pure intentions. Deep-seated love and peace surrounded the child. No child has flaws but innate love like a blank state. They have no words and no chapters to their lives. Endless, explored, experience enters a child's life, to add meaning. This baby was inherently pure. The jutting hand of the baby, protruding out of the mothers wound, was a symbol of an innocent angel.

This slumbering child was hidden inside its home. It dwelled in the spiritual realm of a mother's womb. The womb manifested into a home of warmth and security. An innocent child lacks the state of Id and ego. However, this child was hindered and perturbed by the evil world, which the mother inhabited. The child spontaneously bloomed out of the mother's womb by jabbing its arm through the wound. Its hand touched the atmosphere of a contaminated, corrupt, and guile world of sinners.

"Doctor, please give her a C-section," a relative was desperate.

"If I give her a C-section the baby may live but she will die," it was sad to deliver any negative news.

"Why?" he looked worried.

"We have no blood, if she needs a blood transfusion," I was concerned about medical complications.

"The government did not send blood doctor?" he was aware of the modus operandi of the government.

"Yes, she already lost blood through her wounds," my heightened insight kicked in.

"I do not want to lose her and the baby," he was desperate.

"I understand," I showed empathy.

Grief surrounded me, and I had no emotional space to vent my feelings. I understood their feelings of bereavement. Death did not provide us with an agenda or timetable. In a state of grief, I yearned for my family. Traumatic stress set in when my mind flashed back to the birth of my daughter. I had an acute vision of my newborn daughter, as my eyes locked into the hand of the baby. My own baby's vision emerged into my mind. I was overwhelmed with bittersweet images. Grief surrounded me like an army, ready to take control. Grief was a sniper who held a gun to my head. I looked like a jumbo shrimp ready to give into grief. Ironically, the civil war took place in my head. It was a battle with my logic and my emotional dialogue. Grief did not schedule an appointment with me. Like a mortar shell, grief embedded itself in my mind. My mind was a juxtaposition of the civil war, between the government and the Tamil civilians. I felt empathy for this pregnant woman and her baby, because it reminded me of the birth of my baby daughter. I had to endure the pain and prolonged grief because the last time I saw my daughter, she was only three months old. Six months passed by like the speed of a concord plane.

I took the pregnant woman into the makeshift surgery place. My emotions were still in process.

Empathy emerged, which evoked a sense of pathos. I was the chief doctor in charge of the government hospital, yet my life became so complicated. Each time I took a patient into the operating area, I had to express my condolences and resort to counselling. The pain and grief were acute.

Life did not serve its purpose for this child. The unborn baby was hit by shrapnel from the mortar shells. The baby was not given the opportunity to rejoice on the Earth's sphere. I delved deep down into my philosophical side to analyze the situation. I swallowed several lumps in my throat, as if I was swallowing golf balls. The family was in a state of bereavement. The walls of grief caved in on me.

"The baby died," the family echoed.

"Yes," my words took a leave of absence.

"They killed the baby," I heard a chorus.

"Who?" they established their own philosophical views.

"The government soldiers... our Sri Lankan government army killed the baby," the family wagged their fingers as they spoke in a chorus.

"Yes, they terminated the pregnancy," I spoke with anguish and grief.

The baby was an innocent soul, who was not given the opportunity to take its first breath of air outside the womb. The Sri Lankan army waged a war against an innocent fully developed fetus. They spontaneously killed an innocent fetus, who had no power to fight back. It constitutes murder. In a moral sense that fetus had life. The morality of the philosophical argument is that the army took away the life of a fully developed baby. It is a matter of prolife and human rights. The Sri Lankan army murdered a fetus, a human being. In the case of human rights, the baby a biological human, had every right to live. It was the invasion of a woman's womb. The army invaded the home of the baby, the womb, to terrorize the fetus. The beat of the baby's heart seized to exist. The infant's death was unjustifiable. The womb was the baby's playground. It was a safe haven, for the child to kick as if playing a game of soccer. The womb was its bedroom, where it spent hours of sleeping in peace. The baby's sense of hearing was evoked by the sweet tone of the mother's voice.

That baby was not a fetus soldier, who was manipulated to use a rifle to fight back, from its virtual sensory playground. The noises from the outside world that transmitted through the amniotic fluid, was high frequency sounds. The sounds of guns, rifles, and mortar shells enhanced the spatial growth of the fetus. It was the case of human foils, against human rights.

The baby jabbed its fist through the mothers wound, in the belly. The baby's clenched fist was symbolic of solidarity and support for the Tamil civilians. The baby's raised fist symbolized unity and strength against all opposing forces. The raised clenched fist was a power salute. The baby's clenched fist gestured life, liberty and democracy. The baby protested for human rights, which was an overly political action against the Sri Lankan government. The power salute was a salute to human rights. A fetus raised its clench fist to fight against the oppression of Tamil civilians.

The visual impact of the baby's pumped fist will always symbolize solidarity, against the oppressed Tamil civilians of Sri Lanka.

"How do you know that the mother was attacked by shelling from the Sri Lankan army?" I uttered.

"We are not stupid people. The sound of the shelling and the direction it came from told us if it was sent by the government army or the LTTE soldiers. Even a baby could tell the sound of the shelling from the government army and the LTTE. We could hear the direction it came from. The weapons from both sides were fired differently," a family member enunciated.

"Yes, I totally agree. Even the way it exploded was uniquely different," I articulated.

"Doctor that's how we knew that she and the baby was hit by shelling from the government army," he disclosed.

"No doubt about that," I vocalized.

"A baby brings joy, peace and love into this world," he hollered.

"Yes, now we are faced with torment and fear," I proclaimed.

Torment took control over my mind, body and soul. Torment made me miserable. Watching mass deaths and injury put me into a state of algopsychalia and psychalgia. It was mental anguish and torment. Torment inflicted induced physical, social, psychological, cognitive and emotional pain in me. It was an act of cruelty and degraded my professional performance as a doctor. After the baby's death my mind sang another melancholy melody.

The warmth of the mother's womb,

Turned into a deadly tomb,

The army's shelling was massive,

In the womb the baby was passive,

Waiting for the baby to arrive,

Yet the baby was not alive,

War against a baby is insanity,

It is the evil of all humanity,

The baby was not given security,

Not given the chance for maturity,

A baby left in a state of hunger,

Deprived of food by the war monger,

It is a case of infant mortality,

The army personified immorality,

The baby cried out for compassion,

Yet murdered in a brutal fashion,

A high velocity explosive mortar shell,

Turned the mother's womb into hell,

Bang, bang, bang, bang, bang, bang!

In the air the mortar shells rang,

The emotions of the mother were tense,

The poor baby with no defence,

The womb was symbolic of a crèche,

The shrapnel tore through the flesh,

It's time to turn on the spotlights,

And time to call upon human rights,

The antagonist has to pay the price,

For sending off the shelling device,

Shrapnel cut the mother like a knife,

And painfully the baby lost its life,

Government army performed an abortion,

Their misleading account is distortion,

An army that revealed apathy,

Human Rights promotes empathy.

Like an electric shock my mind jolted back to reality, as the next wounded civilian came in. My heart rate increased, and I went into fight or flight mode. My adrenaline levels rushed like a freight train. My heart rate was like a roller coaster ride. I huffed, and I puffed as my breath increased. My heart beat was rapid like a musician's drums. All the patients around me felt the same distress. I locked eyes with the severely wounded patient. She incited trauma, fear, and anxiety in all the patients. I felt paranoid because I could not believe what I was seeing. The patient was a threat to all of us. She was an inciting force who brought us closer to death.

She was the trigger who put us in danger. I could not envision what would happen to all of us. I had to desensitize all my feelings. Since there was active firing going on all around us the patients and their relatives had to remain horizontal. She elicited fear in all the patients around. The other patients were engaged in a flight mode. It was a frightening situation. I felt a cascade of raw emotions. We perceived danger.

"Doctor do we run," a patient's eyes were wide.

"No," my vision scanned the field.

"We are all going to die," another saw potential danger.

"It's ok," my pupils dilated.

"No, it's not," another doctor scanned the environment.

"Think fast," I rubbed my clammy palms.

"We have a walking time bomb," the doctor perceived danger.

The escalation of violence was evident as airstrikes were rife. A mortar projectile passed through the woman, but it failed to explode. The shell was employed. It pierced through the woman's lower body but did not detonate. It looked as if a broom stick had penetrated her body, with a hazardous mortar shell at the end of the stick. She was a weapon, which placed us at risk. The projectile penetrated her lower abdomen and lodged itself in her.

She resembled cupid, with an arrow through her body. Cupid's arrow delivered love. This arrow delivered hatred. It was an offensive weaponry that could detonate at any time. It was as if she was part of the improvised explosive shell. She did not perish. She was an unexploded ordnance, who arrived at the makeshift hospital. Ironically, it was a no fire zone. She posed as an insurgent. She was alive but covered in blood. It was my prerogative to save her live, with the risk of losing mine.

This was war afflicted against humanity. It was war against the civilians. The mortality rate was high. The government declared active war against the Tamil civilians. We did not have enough blood transfusions for these civilian casualties. The armed conflict targeted civilians. The hospital was a morbid visual situation.

"She needs to be transported to a trauma hospital immediately," I ordered.

"Shock, fear, and coagulopathy will set in due to severe blood loss," another doctor proclaimed.

"Hypothermia, acidosis and dilutional coagulopathy is prone to set in," I explored all issues of medical factors.

"Yes, for sure the need of crystalloids. The plasma-poor blood factors when replacing is also a medical factor," the other doctor acknowledged.

"First… first… first… we need to call in an LTTE soldier to detonate this motor shell, or our lives are at stake… and the patients too…," I stuttered.

"We can save her life. We just need immediate cooperation," the other doctor was nervous.

"Blood transfusion is needed… whole blood, red blood cells and the fresh frozen plasma, is a must," I explored all medical avenues.

We were in a challenging, critical, combat zone. I was afraid that she would hemorrhage. We needed a lot of blood transfusion products. This case was extreme. It validated that Tamil civilians were targeted. The civilians suffered injuries from shells, explosives, firearms, blasts, shrapnel and other explosive materials. Men, woman and mostly children suffered extreme injuries to the spine, abdomen, head, thorax, and musculoskeletal injuries. Then there were those who ruthlessly perished.

The situation and atmosphere were a total dystopia. It was a humanitarian concern because innocent civilians were explicitly targeted. There were thousands of civilian casualties rather than combatant casualties. The killings of civilians were intentional and brutal, which constituted genocide. These Tamil civilians were legitimate targets. It was obvious that their human rights were violated. The elderly, handicap, innocent children and woman were butchered. It was a waging and raging battle against innocent Tamil civilians. They were legitimate targets, who were not attributed moral rights. Tamil civilians were targeted in the no fire zones.

A baby, fetus and aging grandmother became combatants. That was the immoral conduct of the civil war in Sri Lanka. A baby's pumped fist through the walls of the womb, validates the collapsed morale. A fetus as a legitimate target was unethical.

The woman who looked like an antique, vintage, primitive hobby horse, lived to tell her inhumane tale. She arrived at the hospital resembling a stick, play, hobby horse. The head of the horse was the deadly mortar shell. The body of the horse resembled a broom stick. The riding horse stick was like a sphere, which penetrated her soul. The idiom to "ride a hobby horse," speculated on following one's goals in life or hobby.

From a modern perspective this Tamil civilian did not perceive carrying a deadly mortar shell as a hobby.

"So, she was safe at the hospital. The bomb was deactivated. I could have saved her life... saved her legs. I heard through the grape vine that the doctors at the regional hospital amputated her legs," I shed tears of joy.

"Yes, gangrene or malignancy could have set in. She was in severe trauma... but thanks God... she survived such a traumatic ordeal," the other doctor gave a sign of relief.

"She is in recovery now. We could have performed the operation here if we had proper medical tools and medication. I did not approve of her legs being amputated. But if it had to be done..." my thoughts ran deep.

"That's ok... now let's go and save more lives," my colleague was sincere.

I felt as if I was in a carousel of death. It was like a merry-go-round of gloom. I visualized myself sitting on the wooden horse, elevated on a post. My simulated galloping motion took me around the circumference. It was not the circumference of a brightly lit playground. I clung to the handle of life, while revolving around the circle of death. I jostled with death. I spun around a menagerie of injured civilians. My head progressed clockwise, while my body lugged counter clockwise. As my imaginary carrousel gained momentum, I was not delighted by the prominent sight of blood. The carousel of doom exposed more than 300 000 injured Tamil civilians, most on the brink of death.

Instead of riding the carousel of joy, fun, excitement and social interactions, I rode the carousel of mistrust, shame, doubt and guilt. Each time my patients gave in to death, I had to tolerate failure. The carousel reinforced torment, as I spun around observing hungry and lifeless bodies.

CHAPTER 3

In the Shadow of Death

      Death challenged my desires and instincts. Working at the hospital was traumatic. Death was a regular visitor at the hospital. He was bold and manipulative. Death did not align with my altruistic nature. Death replaced compassion, kindness and love with grief, stress, and chaos. He wanted me to evict my soul. My soul was deeply embedded in its luxury home, my body. Evicting my soul meant giving in to death. I played a game of tug-of-war with death. The hospital was bleak, yet treating patients was my passion in life. Death delivered trauma and torment.

The government delivered medicine via the Red Cross ship. The doctors ordered one hundred thousand to three thousand antibiotics. That was barely enough to treat patients for a period of two or three days. They hoodwinked the foreign media and the foreign countries by informing them that they sent the doctors sufficient medication. It was as if the foreign countries viewed the civil war in Sri Lanka with blind folds on. The Sri Lankan government called the bluff and played a game of hocus-pocus with any foreign intervention. It was a great government strategy to hoodwink foreigners about the civil war.

The doctors and Tamil civilian casualties were not bamboozled by the Sri Lankan government's manipulation and deceptive operation. We lacked basic facilities like laboratories to do blood and urine tests. We had no x-ray laboratories and x-rays, mammograms and gastrointestinal tract. There was no equipment to help the doctors diagnose the war casualties' injuries. Antibiotics, injections and pain medication were limited.

"Do we have any anaesthesia and blood banks," a frustrated doctor was in a state of panic.

"More than 100 patients are injured in this war. How do we perform surgeries?" it was a rhetorical question from another doctor.

"After the surgeries the patients are sent to the other hospitals. For God sake they can see what we need and what we do," I held back my anger.

"Well the LTTE sector sent us some anaesthesia and other supplies to perform surgeries," my associate doctor gave a sign of relief.

"The Sri Lankan government lied to the media and foreign agencies that the LTTE is stealing the medication that they sent us. That's a dirty lie. There is no truth in that. They are dodging the gun. The government is blaming the LTTE for their own deceptions," my tormented mind lashed out.

"Yes, they lied to foreign media that they killed the LTTE... They killed innocent Tamil civilians... especially Tamil women and children," my doctor colleague vented.

"They attended the market and blatantly lied that the LTTE killed the civilians, who went to the market to do their shopping," I dabbled with the truth.

"I was there at the market. I witnessed this first hand. It was during the sundry period," I continued as I was brutally honest.

We did not have any anaesthesia and blood vials. The situation at the hospital was a total pandemonium. Turmoil chaos and confusion was the prominent atmosphere. It was a state of hell, created by the human antagonist. The hospital turned into a bloody black dungeon. Satan played a game of cops and robbers with us. Those who died followed the golden pavement and entered the bright light of heaven.

The irony of the situation was that we cried hysterically as each person passed on. However, the dead were transported in a carriage to a world of happiness, in the arms of God. In fact the dead cried for us because we were in the centre of Hell, a place surrounded by pandemonium. Black shadows hung upon the hospital. Satan fired his fiery, bludgeoned arrow causing mayhem.

The LTTE sent us medication but we used minimum dosage to treat the patients. Pain medication was limited. I did massive surgeries like amputations, with limited anaesthesia and painkillers. Hundreds of civilians came to us because they were injured by shells, sent by the military. We could not discriminate. We had to treat anyone who entered the hospital. As a medical doctor, I took a pledge to treat the ill and injured. Both the injured LTTE and the injured government military could enter the hospital for treatment.

We had about three hundred thousand population. However, the government confirmed that there were only eighty thousand people. That formed the criteria for them to reduce the medication sent to us. Ironically, the medication and food delivered to the hospital were not for eighty thousand people. It was a cruel game of Russian roulette. The Sri Lankan government spun the cylinder of lies and deception. They pulled the trigger, while pointing the gun at our heads. Each bullet in the chamber was a threat and a manipulation tactic, in the revolver of life. The Sri Lankan military played a game of Russian roulette with our futures.

"Did we get any food," the patient's stomach growled like a rabid dog.

"They only sent food for 5000 people," I also felt the desire to eat.

"We ran out of food. I am also hungry," I felt sympathy and empathy, for the patient.

I looked around and the situation constituted civilians yearning for food and suffering from hunger pangs.

I worked in several hospitals. All the hospitals were attacked by the government army.

"We declared the GPS coordination to the government, to notify them of the exact location of all the hospitals," a Red Cross member was precise.

"I went to all corners of the hospital to provide a GPS coordination," I assured him.

"No, no, no!" another doctor colleague retorted.

"Yes, I did give them," I argued.

"Yes, he did," the Red Cross member validated.

The argument was based on the government's evil actions. The day after the GPS coordination was handed to the government military personal, the hospital was precisely shelled. All the hospitals were attacked. The government army was about eight hundred metres surrounding the hospital. They observed the hospital with intensity, observing people who entered or left. Shelling the hospital was not an accident. It was intentional. The Ministry of health, Humanitarian Organizations and the Government military were all blatantly advice on the exact location of the hospitals. The government army was well equipped with contemporary sources to monitor the surroundings. They are not a primitive army but an excellent trained army for combat. Their combat training, as soldiers was advanced.

"We are a military target," a member of the Red Cross confirmed.

"How do we fight back, with blood vials, callipers, champs, dilators, forceps, gags, gouges, forceps, retractors, curettes and other surgical instruments. This is total insanity," I found it difficult to digest such illogical attacks from the military.

"The Red Cross is present as our witness," my colleague validated.

"They lied that the LTTE was firing from inside the hospital. How ludicrous can that be?" I laughed.

"Totally absurd," my colleague added.

"They know where the hospitals are. They have advanced satellite planes to distinguish our locations," I noted.

"Yes, they have good sources to figure out who and what their targets where," my colleague yelled with disbelief.

"They are such liars. They said that if the LTTE is firing from the hospital, then they have to retaliate. The Red Cross members are here to witness such lies. They are lying … such liars," my emotions ran high.

The Sri Lankan government was confronted by the international community. They blatantly lied that they did not know there were hospitals in the area. It was a total paradox, when the government military gave another story. The government military confessed that they accidentally shelled the hospital. They were caught in a web of lies. Like a spider they spun their web of lies to manipulate the foreign media. Like a fly they got caught in their own web of lies. They did not perceive the consequences of their own lies. The Sri Lankan government manipulated the truth. Their deliberate distortion of the truth tangled them in a web of lies. It was as if they were in an obstacle course, jumping over the hurdle of truth. The government ran through a maze of deceit, that they could not find the end.

Deceits lead to confusion. The Red Cross provided confirmation that there were no LTTE points inside or close to the hospital. The government wanted me to carry their baton like a relay race and carry the fake news to the media. That was not the Olympic relay race of track and field. I was not going to use the symbolic baton of lies to pass on the fake message. The audio point of the firing came from five hundred meters, in the direction of the government army.

Ironically, since I swore to tell the truth and nothing but the truth, the government officials made me look like a village idiot, in front of the media. *Some village has lost its idiot*, I thought.

"The shelling came from 500 meters, in the direction of the government military. They targeted the hospital," I took a note, from the no fire zone.

"Sorry sir, he does not know what he is saying. He misinterpreted your question," a government official interjected.

The government official made me look like a moron. They created their own story. They designed their own worksheet, with their own questions and answers. This was a new form of media literacy. The government did not want to deliver the truth. They tried to edit my mouth. They tried to shrink the truth. They threatened me.

The visual sights of injuries, blood, deaths and torture tormented me. I hold thousands of stories in my heart. With each heartbeat, I am able to release a story of torture and death. With each breath I take, I fight for human rights. This is a note from the no fire zone.

Mental and physical trauma followed me around like a shadow. One gruesome night I was doing my rounds at the hospital, with all my altruistic traits. I began my rounds on the lower level. I planned to stop by on the children's ward to monitor the children. It was about 7pm. I wanted to progress to the woman's ward. Disaster struck because I had a complicated delivery.

"Doctor this is a complicated delivery," the nurse was in a state of panic.

"Do you need help," my altruistic trait set in.

"Yes, please doctor," her voice was urgent.

"Hold on, I will be there soon," I reassured her.

I heard a loud bang. It was as if the earth moved. The hospital was shelled. The shell fell into the pediatric and woman's ward. It was a bittersweet moment because the shell had just missed me. I skipped that ward to head to the labour ward. It was a notion of serendipity and synchronicity. It was as if my soul propelled me in another direction. The Universe aligned the nine planets in that critical moment. My spiritual path led me away from destruction. As a man of science, I had to dabble with its elusive sense. I chanted my mantra, to thank my guardian angel, for sparing my life. The universe knew that I was there to help, heal, harmonize, and resuscitate patients.

Suddenly, the lights went off and I was surrounded by menacing darkness. I was surrounded by blackness. The lights were off, but my heart was illuminated with empathy. Darkness caved unto me. Darkness was the monster that prevented me from proceeding with my medical duties. Death accompanied darkness, disaster, destruction, devastation and a demonic presence. Darkness encompassed an atmosphere of fear and chaos. I felt the presence of Satan in action. Darkness visited the hospital with negative destruction. The universe delivered spiritual darkness. I could not walk in darkness, because I had to illuminate the truth.

In the western culture people would perceive darkness as a Halloween night. I could not conceive what was going on around me. I felt as if blood sucking vampires touched my face. Darkness continued to lurk around like a burglar waiting to steal my logic. My body propelled me towards fight or flight mode. My mind brewed a concoction of an evil stew. However, I had no control over my impulses. My internal battle was worse than my external chaos. My body had a chemical reaction. My body released norepinephrine, which caused my heart and muscles to contract. My heart beat was rapid. My breathing was intense. I felt as if I was in a horror movie.

I felt goosebumps as I stepped onto a gooey monster. I had to monitor my own heart and respiratory rate. I endured psychological torment. My own body played games with me. I felt a sloppy, mawkish and sticky fluid on my leg. It was greasy. It was like slime. Each time I attempted to pick up my foot, the nectar sap tugged at my foot. It was as if I was held prisoner in a new dimension of aliens. An alien vessel had entered the hospital. A creepy, crawly, slimy creature was crawling up my leg.

Hysterical cries filled the air. Emotion disturbance was evident.

"Help me."

"Help me please,"

"Amma, amma, amma help."

"Appa, appa, appa, appa!"

"I'm dying…"

"No… no… no… ahhhh!"

"Ammama… no ammama!"

"Appapa… appapa… appapa…."

"Don't go… don't go!"

"Don't leave me please!"

"Anna, Akka…"

Chilling, gut wrenching cries surrounded me. They were cries of desperation. They were cries of death. They were cries of separation anxiety.

Assistants sped in with flash lights. The flash lights illuminated the wards. It was as if these flash lights eliminated the evil forces. The illuminated lights spiritually symbolized purity, power, and good over evil, for all Hindus. Good triumphs over all evil.

I looked around and I was surrounded by blood, body parts and dead bodies. The slime that I trampled on were body parts, human organs and dead bodies. The roof caved in. Some walls caved in. The ward was exposed to the starry sky. The next day the Red Cross members arrived to clean the blood and help fix the roof. They used a temporary tarp to fix the roof.

Unfortunately, the next night the government army shelled the operating theatre. They did it again. It was on February 3, that our operating theatre was fully destroyed. Together with my medical colleagues, we cleaned the operation theatre. Seven patients waited in line for their operations. The door of the operation theatre perished. Body parts flew all over the room. I was mentally tormented to witness such a horrific sequence of events. Yet it was my note, from the no fire zone.

A dedicated nurse, who demonstrated kindness and embodied all core values, was present. She personified dignity and integrity. Altruism followed her like a shadow. She held the hand of an old lady and engaged in attaching an intravenous (IV) to her vein. When the ward was shelled by the army, she died, still holding the hand of the gentle lady. It was a sight that is deeply embedded in my mind. The imagery follows me around. She was a young nurse. She did not live to tell her story.

Death surrounded me. Civilians died in the hospitals, homes, streets, church, temples, mosque and every environment. It was a carousel of death. An ocean of dead people surrounded us. The cessation of their heartbeat was impossible. I looked around and spiritually conceived that their souls, said its last goodbyes, to journey to a more integral realm, where peace and prosperity prevails. The astral projection must have been a sad story, when disembodiment was captured. Other souls remain surfing on a grey cloud above. The manifestation of such brutal deaths leaves some souls in a state of confusion. The energy of the soul's spirit lingers on in a new spiritual realm. The soul enters the golden light. The unresolved issues on earth are Human Rights. Humans project as antagonists. They believe that they have the power to kill. Human nature can be so evil. It is time human beings seek pure and true harmony. Human beings need to create their own dharma to progress towards light. They need to address all aspects of karma. When there is tragedy, people get together in unity to celebrate the life of the dead. Human beings need to unite in good spirits to celebrate life on earth, the life of the living.

People visited churches and temples to pray to God to save their lives, yet it is in those religious institutions that they died. It torments me. I need to hold onto the tormenting incidents to make the world aware of such human genocide. Mentally, I made a note of what went on, in the NO FIRE ZONE.

The incident that broke my heart was when a twelve-year-old girl, gracefully entered the hospital with her eight-year-old sister. They lost their parents through the army shelling. They were both innocent souls who tried to give new meaning to a world, without parents. The twelve-year-old girl assumed the role of a surrogate parent to her eight-year-old sister. The eight-year-old was hit by a shell. Her brain oozed out of her head. Both beautiful butterflies did not perceive the dangers of such an injury. They were lost. Naively, innocence followed them around like Mary's Little lamb, the nursery rhyme embedded in every kindergarten's mind. They lacked wisdom, manifested through experience and judgement.

Medically, I was aware that the eight-year-old would die within minutes. Within minutes she would be brain death. In the depth of my heart I could not tell the twelve-year-old that her sister was going to die. They had been through trauma with the death of their parents.

"Doctor please save my sister," innocence surrounded her.

"Yes, yes, yes!" I tried to sound optimistic.

"Doctor I only have my sister," she cried.

"Yes! I know," I played the paternal role.

"Promise me doctor," she needed affirmation.

"Certainly," I was in a position of role play.

"I cannot be alone," she was fighting death.

"You will not be alone," my voice projected kindness.

I knew she was going to die. The eight-year-old developed a sudden and violet seizure. Her convulsion was acute.

"Doctor please, please help her," she cried with empathy.

"No, doctor, take her into the operating room and give her surgery," she fought for her sister's life.

"OK," I was calm, yet my heart sank with grief.

I felt as if I was on stage, in a play. I had to role play to comfort the twelve-year-old. I acted as if I gave the eight-year-old medicine, to calm the twelve-year-old, who had such persuasive skills. She eventually died in her sisters' arms. I cried to witness such innocence.

"She is dead doctor," she sounded like an adult.

"Ummm," my vice took a leave of absence.

"I have to bury her body doctor," a child who did not know how to take care of adult duties.

"Everything is OK," I calmed her.

My heart sank like the Titanic ship. I thought about my child. The universe placed the 12-year-old in a world surrounded by evil. She was all alone and confused. She was an angel, who was in shock. She envisioned living life alone and taking care of her eight-year-old sister. She was alone, a twelve-year-old girl left to fend for herself. Other adults at the hospital surrounded her with love, kindness and compassion. This twelve-year-old girl implanted a seed of compassion in my heart. This is what the government army did to a little girl. Her human rights were violated.

My mind was tormented, as it sang a song of compassion and love.

Two beautiful monarch butterflies,

The tormented sister's loud cries,

Two innocent children in need,

In my heart they planted a seed,

In their faces I saw my child,

My emotions grew brutally wild,

They held on to each other's love,

Their deceased parents were above,

Two children in the world alone,

Heart of the soldier made of stone,

Declaring war against two sisters,

Their fragile hearts covered with blisters,

As young as only twelve and eight,

But surrounded by evil and hate,

A serious matter of human rights,

Children left with sleepless nights,

Observing the fear in their eyes,

Surrounded by manipulation and lies,

The brutal death of their mom and dad,

And losing her sister made her mad,

Then born into the Tamil culture,

Preyed upon by a vulture,

Declaring war against civilians,

Preaching lies on media pavilions,

A child became a surrogate mother,

Because she was left with no other,

Innocent children orphaned by war,

And stranded at the hospital door,

An adult world they had to explore,

The act of violence they deplore,

Being indoctrinated by troops,

Dangers faced by armed groups,

Torment and psychological stress,

A brutal life I have to confess,

The parent was the human shield,

Children isolated in a dangerous field,

She did not want her sister to die,

She was not ready to say goodbye,

A twelve-year-old left to grieve,

So humble, innocent and naïve,

Did not know how to bury her body,

Without family she was nobody,

Declaring war against a child,

Humanitarian case has to be filed,

It's all about political tension,

We need to attract world attention,

A child took a bullet to the head,

A child that was left brain dead,

The body of the parents under rubble,

A child left in a dangerous bubble.

Human rights look at this case!

All began in the government army base,

Tamil civilians in need of cremations,

Attention needed by the United Nations.

I saved lives. However, I could have saved more lives if only I was given proper medical tools, medical equipment, medication and upgraded medical facilities. We were plagued by the torment of war. We were not given justice. As a doctor my personal safety was at risk. Physically, my presence at the hospital was jeopardized by shelling. Socially, I was isolated from my nuclear and extended family. Psychologically, I was tormented by the Sri Lankan government to lie to the international media.

I was the prime witness, who encountered all the suffering and torment of war. The international world humanitarian organizations needed to digest the story from the civilian perspective. The matter could not be addressed lightly. A person or media hoodwinked by lies from the Sri Lankan government are victims themselves. The massive killing of Tamil civilians cannot be brushed off like dusting dandruff off the shoulders. The government lies is like bacterial fungal with scaly stories, which needs to be treated.

This was war crime and genocide. We craved for a political solution. At the same time, we craved for food. Like a butler delivering food, I wanted to deliver my story on a silver platter to the United Nations. I was the victim of political abuse. Tamils continue to suffer.

The government army overpowered the Tamil civilians. The Tamil lands, homes, and temples where confiscated. The government put on a brilliant façade in front of the international organizations, as a pretence that they are safe guarding the rights of all Tamil nationals in Sri Lanka. The visual imagery created by the government is a masquerade ball. Like a magician they have a cloak over the genocide of Tamil civilians. It is deception, hypocrisy and a total paradox. The veil had to be lifted and truth unveiled. A peaceful country does not require the presence of an army in Tamil residential region. Young girls and women feared their safety when walking around at night. The army poses as a threat to their existence. Freedom without fear and intimidation was what they craved for.

The army influence in the north and east was relentless. They influence the routine daily activity of the Tamil civilians. The ratio of the army to civilians is five army soldiers to one Tamil civilians, which is absurd.

As a witness I was forced to answer close ended questions. These questions do not illicit an explanation but a yes or no response. The Lesson Learnt and Reconciliation Commission, is a commission of inquiry mandated to release factual information about the civil war. I was suppressed from narrating my real factual account on humanitarian grounds. My rights were violated, against the policy of the international humanitarian law.

I witnessed who was responsible for the shelling of hospitals and the numbers of Tamil civilians' casualties. As a witness, I did not receive any protection. I am forced to zip my mouth and throw away the key. In doing so, I emerge as a tormented doctor, carrying the burden of that brutal imagery in the NO FIRE ZONE. What I observe is not a hyperbole. It is a verbal visual essay sketched in my mind. It is the unedited version of the brutal truth.

I had fundamental rights in the war zone. The hospitals had to operate according international protocol. When the international organizations were asked to leave, the Tamil civilians were vulnerable to more attacks. There were no foreign bystanders to provide a witness testimony. The international foreigner proved to be a credible witness.

My witness account was subject to manipulation, not through my own inner bias, but through interrogation to conceal the truth. My eyes were symbolic of the lenses of a movie camera. It recorded all the activity around me. It captured the moving images and saved them in my cognitive frame. My eyes were a Go Pro, mounted on my face that captured every moving story around the hospital. My video footage is captured in my mind. My record button was on at all times. My vision was ultra-wide, with a 360° angle view. With vivid sharpness I captured every scene. I encountered thousands of brutal images from my unique perspective, the compressed video file. I monitored every brutal scene, with extreme sharpness. My voice is the digital audio that would generate the digital sound, with the vivid rendering images.

The neo cortex of my brain associated with reasoning is my zoom lens, with a wide range. It had equivalent range to capture the visual pictures of the sight and sound of the shelling.

I did not fail to protect the Tamil civilians. I failed to speak up and explore the truth in front of the international media. It is an appearance, verses reality. The brutal shelling of innocent Tamil civilians is just spectacular, sensational, secretive news to the outside world. News is entertainment in today's society. However, when a person's family member is brutally killed, it unfolds into reality. These Tamil civilians were symbolic of my wife, child, mother, father and extended family unit. They were not just part of the news. When the television set is turned off people forget about the news and progress to sleep. What if the person on the news is their family member, they have sleepless nights and nightmares.

A family collapses with death and devastation. We cannot replace the life our loved ones. The civilians lost their land, houses, personal property and family members. The loss was profound. Civilians were placed in IDP camps, with no mobility. Tamil civilians who were displaced from their homes were sent to Internally Displaced Persons Camp (IDP) in Vanni.

A doctor who wrote an article about the IDP and the army's offensive behaviour became a target. The Sri Lankan government preyed him on like a lion stalking its prey.

I am a witness. I am the ultimate GoPro. I can tread the path of this earth and deliver my account in any country. I do not have a witness protection in Sri Lanka. I have no security. I can be killed. The shelling prevented many civilians from seeking help at the hospitals. The road became a cemetery. The road was the ultimate grave yard. More than forty thousand people must have died due to shelling. It is possible to gain the precise data of the dead.

According to the United Nations report, the death toll was about forty thousand. The missing could also be dead.

In Mullaitivu the hospital was an old ruin, a displaced school building. There were only two washrooms. Two washrooms served hundreds of injured civilians. I served under dangerous conditions. In 2009 we got allocations from the health ministers. We had to get the clearance from the military. We did not have enough wards. We faced devastating problems. We had not enough water supplies. Problems walked around the school building like a principal making his rounds, throughout the school. We sent about four hundred patients to other surrounding hospitals. Problems walked around the school like teachers, teaching us to be strong, self-sufficient and independent. Problems taught us to delve deep down into our inner-self to find self-confidence. The problems became our fundamental teachers. Problems taught us to be innovative and to find solutions.

CHAPTER 4

The Shelling Continued

I walked around the hospital observing patients. In the depth of silence, I found wisdom. It was 3pm. I had my last meal at 11pm. We ran out of food and I was hungry. My intuitive wisdom told me that the government had their own agenda by not sending us food. I nurtured my intuition and saw beyond the illusions of the civil war. I explored the fact that the Tamil civilian casualties could die of starvation.

It was May 14, 2009, a day I could reckon with. I delved deep down into the motives of the government. I could hear the shelling. The government army fired at the LTTE as they retreated, they were approaching the hospital. The shelling got louder. My intuition told me that it was a sign of impeding danger. The situation around me was bleak.

To take our minds of our hunger pangs, we needed a comic relief. Our dramatic tension was released when the doctors at the hospital joked.

"I wonder which one of us will be picked up by the white van, as a political prisoner!" I foreshadowed.

"Lots of ethic Tamils and journalists have been picked up by the secretive white van... and you're next doctor," my doctor colleague joked.

"The white van is coming for us," another colleague laughed.

"The mysterious white van will pick you up and disappear," I was sarcastic.

"Yes, that white van is the boogie man," another colleague was animated.

"When the courier delivers the next mortar shell, please go out and check whose name is on it," we laughed.

The white van was no joke. In fact, the white van was a terrorist van. It belonged to the Sri Lankan government and the government army. The white van was a symbol of political motivation. Anyone, who spoke up against the government or about the government activities, was kidnapped by the white van. They were brutally assaulted by the military and some were left to die. It is apparent that when they were kidnapped, they had no contact with their family and friends.

The men who were kidnapped by the white van were taken to an unknown location, where they were brutally raped and tortured. They were branded with cigarettes by the captors. They were beaten. These perpetrators removed the clothing of the Tamil men and violently raped them. Some were raped using broom sticks and barbed wire, which resulted in internal bleeding. Rape torture and branding were the modus operandi of the military perpetrators. The bureaucratic process was not fair to victims. They denied claims of a white van, which kidnapped Tamils. They claimed that white vans were owned by civilians. The victims were expected to remember the registration number of the white van. Victims suffered violent rape, sodomy, oral copulation, branding assaults, kidnapping and life in prison. The culmination of such violence is against all human rights. The ordeal caused the victims to experience psychological trauma and nightmares. Those who lived to tell their stories, still suffer physically, socially and psychologically. The white van is a symbol of torture. The occupants of the white van went against all the criteria set by the Human Rights organization.

Mullivaikal east hospital was in a dangerous setting. It was surrounded by the navy and army. Shells flew over the hospital. Several staff and patients were killed by shelling. Due to the shelling everyone in the hospital had to crawl. We could not walk. Doctors crawled around like crabs. Sometimes we crawled like army snipers. Other times we exhibit an infant crawl. I propelled myself around the hospital like a crab, treating patients. Ironically, the newly injured who arrived at the hospital for treatment were killed by the army shelling and gun shots.

At a certain stage we had eighty dead bodies. However, the families could not remove the bodies from the hospital due to the shelling. It was a "no movement zone". There were no mortuaries. The situation was morbid. There were no ankle bracelets, toe tags or metal chilled trays. Bodies were lowered into the sand at the school compound, in mass burials with several human corpses. It was not cruelty but a sanitation factor, in war conflict. May 14, 2009 was literally dooms day.

"What do I do?" I phoned the LTTE Health Leader.

"What are conditions like?" he asked.

"Patients are dying by the minute. They are being shelled by the army," I was full of empathy.

"Sounds dangerous," he retorted.

"I do not want to close the hospitals. My duty is to save patients. My patients are important," I signed.

"We respect you for saving patients. You deserve the Maamanithar Award. You are a hero," he praised.

"I need the Red Cross to bring the ship. The government gave us one hour to load the patients onto the Red Cross ship. However, it takes eight hours to transport patients onto the Red Cross ship. If we transport the patients via the road, we have no witness if they are killed," my altruistic nature shone through.

The Red Cross ship anchored on the international waters for three days. The government denied the ship access to the beach.

The doctors and administration staff had a small house-quarters. We had a small well to shower. The army was stationed about 200 meters from our dwelling. The heavy shelling on May 14 prevented us from cooking or eating. Under the clouds of darkness, the army drew near. Like a lion stalking its prey, the army was ready to launch upon us. They were closing in on us as if we were their targeted prey. We were devoid of protection. They were inadvertently close. They utilised their GPS to locate us.

On May 15, 2009 at 3am the fighting subsided. I predicted that the army will reach us around 4 to 5am. At about noon, a Canadian Radio station contacted me.

"Hello!" it was the Canadian Radio Station.

"Hello," I remained motionless like a frightened squirrel.

"You are in danger," he foreshadowed.

"Yes!" I had an erratic quick motion.

"We heard in Canada that the army is going to use poison gas on the Tamil civilians," he had urgency in his voice.

"I did not hear that," I was concerned.

"Yes!" I acknowledge.

"What's your situation?" his concern grew deep.

"It is possible that I am going to die soon. I feel as if they will kill me," I foreshadowed my own death.

I did not eat breakfast, lunch or dinner and I was starving and dehydrated. I was afraid of cognitive impairment. I embraced the feeling of hunger pangs and focused on my patients. The LTTE passed us and we were stationed in the middle of the LTTE and the army.

About ten feet away from me I saw a bright flash. I felt as if death was impending. I encompassed a sensation of detachment. I was going to get water while others were sitting outside. It was as if my body experienced levitation. I was in mid-air doing a barrel roll, like a stunt man. I felt an astral projection. I was rigorously thrown into the air in an iconic fashion. I triumphantly spiralled in the air, as if I was James Bond. The bright light was like a space shuttle launching me into thin air. It was a case of serendipity and a mystic sense. I leaped into the air like a Hollywood star. However, I dropped as if I was bungee jumping. My body travelled with speed. I hit the ground with dynamic speed.

I felt like getting up and announcing to those around me, "My name is Bond... James Bond!" Or maybe! it would have sounded better if I announced, "My name is Varatharajah... Doctor Varatharajah."

However, my arm dislocated from the body. I felt as if my ligaments and tendons tore upon impact.

"Hello Dr. Varatharajah!" the doctors chorused.

"Hello, wake up hello!" there was panic in their voices.

"The government army sent a shell," another retorted.

"Is he going to die?" Another showed concern.

I was in shock. I heard their panic-stricken voices. My voice took a leave of absence, I could not answer. I was in a state of hypovolemic shock. I felt a haemorrhage in my nose. Blood oozed out of my mouth and nose. My arm was numb and outstretched. The direct blow caused a dislocation. My hand was paralyzed. My nostrils accumulated dust. I also sustained two shrapnel wounds in my belly. It was a critical period in my life and I knew that I would die in about ten minutes. It was my golden ten minutes. I had morbid feelings of death where I cried for my wife, child and family. Survival would prolong my suffering. I could not imagine life without my right hand. I was surrounded by my doctor colleagues who provided me with medical interventions. They were not going to allow death to take me away.

The government army knew we were in the doctor's quarters, they chose to bomb it. The fighting continued and grew louder. The empirical commands from the army and LTTE were bombastic and loud.

"Hello Red Cross, we have an injured doctor who was hit by a bomb," my doctor colleague was concerned.

"I am going to die," I cried.

"No, you will be fine," my colleague reassured me.

"Hi Red Cross, can we have a ship to take the injured doctor to safety," he begged.

"No, just go deeper inland," the Red Cross was naive.

"But we are already deep inland," my colleagues pleaded.

'The government army is progressing closer to us," another doctor yelled.

"The army knows our position. Why are they attacking us? Is this intentional?" my doctor colleague was upset.

I knew that I lost my right arm, which caused my anguish. My head could not turn towards my wounded side. A laparotomy was needed. A surgical incision in my abdomen needed to be performed. A tube needed to be inserted to remove the blood from my lungs.

"Where is my arm? Find my arm," I bawled.

"Here is your arm," another doctor placed my dislocated arm across my stomach.

"But there is no sensory movement," I shrieked.

"But a portion is attached," another doctor consoled me.

"I am so thirsty. I need water please!" I hollered.

"You are a doctor. You know water causes more bleeding. How can you ask for water? That's not good for you," my doctor colleague howled like the wind.

"Give me a saline IV to detox my wound and rehydrate me," I bellowed, giving instructions to other doctors was ironic.

"I am going to die. I do not have a right hand," I gave them a hard time.

"Your hand is not totally dislocated. We placed it across your stomach," the other doctor restored my confidence.

"I am sweating. I feel thirsty, hungry and shock," I roared like a lion, as the doctors bandaged me.

I shook violently after the sudden explosion. My mind was traumatised, confused and disturbed. The other doctors called the Red Cross and defence ministry to address the issue.

About 45 minutes after the bomb landed close to me, I struggled with my injuries. The other doctors treated my injuries meticulously. The situation was tense, traumatic, terrible and full of trepidation. We could not figure out the government army's mobilization sequence and strategies. They attacked the host hospital. It was brutal extremism. The doctors and patients were in a state of bewilderment. They could not embrace the fact that a fellow doctor was injured. The bombings and massacre on the Tamil citizens, involved genocide. We were puzzled as to why the army would attack us. We needed a secure shield. The attack to kill me was foiled.

Suddenly, out of the blues, a radical army soldier appeared. I almost jumped out of my skin. He pointed his riffle at us as if we were a pride of lions. We had no vigilant security and the soldier unleashed fear in us.

"Hands up!" he sounded like a violent extremist.

"This doctor is injured. He needs immediate treatment," a doctor was humble.

"Be quiet!" he hailed as an extremist, still pointing his monstrous rifle at us.

"Our doctor and Health directed got an injury. He needs immediate health care. He needs a laparotomy. Please sir help him," my colleague pleaded.

"Ask him to walk towards the army. Damn him. He needs to be killed. He treated the LTTE," he was verbally abusive in the Sinhala language.

"But sir, he is a government doctor. He is a director at the hospital," my colleague showed kinship ties.

"I will kill all of you for treating the LTTE. All of you deserve to die," he treated us if we belonged to a cult membership.

"Please sir, just take me. Leave all the other doctors behind to treat the injured patients. I do not want them to die for me. I will go with you on my own," I was selfless.

"No, we will go with our colleague," they showered loyalty.

"Please be quiet and do not talk to them," I was afraid that the soldier would become aggressive if we spoke too much.

The stress of being in the army took a toll on the soldier's emotional state of mind. His anger was intense and aggressive. He was verbally abusive. His tolerance level was low when we spoke to him. His temper indicated that he would kill us, as the trigger was pointed to our heads. The doctors were overwhelmed with fear. We lived through the bitter, bloody and dark days of the civil war. We were government doctors at the hospital, yet the government adopted a covert attitude towards us. It was a game of "cloak and dagger." We received Tamil civilians who were maimed, mutilated, mangled and incapacitated. I cringed when I thought about senseless genocide, which caved in on us. I was laced with pain. Anxiety, stress and trauma shattered my life. The soldier abusively yelled at us to walk in the direction of the army, into the face of guerrilla warfare. Five doctors were stripped of their dignity, ethical and moral standards. We were unappreciated by a crazed psychopathic government soldier. He was ready to engage in combat and kill us. I sacrificed my family life to treat the wounded Tamil patients, yet I was treated like a criminal. I engaged with the enemy, who thought I was culturally inferior.

Five doctors were ambushed and sent to the foe. My loyal doctor colleagues placed me on a stretcher. The doctors rotated as they carried me through the bushes and muddy roads. The night was dark and there was darkness in my fragile heart. Death came in the form of darkness and I was ready to give in to death. I was on a rudiment makeshift stretcher. If my injury did not kill me, I knew the army would kill me.

I felt as if my stretcher was my casket and my doctor colleagues were my pallbearers. It felt as if they were carrying me to my burial site, with honour and dignity. The atmosphere was dense and sombre. There was no hearse. My pallbearers escorted me over the bumpy terrain, to hand me over to death. I wondered if the obnoxious soldier would deliver my eulogy. My loyal colleagues carried my weight, and I felt the guilt of them bearing the pain. I imagined my wife, child and parents grieving at my grave. The road was long, and the pain was chronic.

Inevitably, walking created dust emissions, through the rural terrain. The unpaved roads were partially muddy. Dirt and dust crept up my nostrils, as if seeking refuge from the army. As we cross another road we came across an army bus. My colleagues tried to halt the bus, with excitement.

"Hello sir, our friend is badly injured. He is a government doctor. Please help transport him to the hospital. He needs immediate surgery," they signed with relief.

"We will not take him into the bloody bus. We will ride this bus over him you idiots," we detected a violent combative atmosphere.

"But sir…," my colleague pleaded.

"Get out of my sight. I will run my bus over your doctor friend and you. You want to die. I will kill all of you. You have no witness. I will run my bus over all of you idiots. Watch me. I am serious you bleep, bleep, bleep, moron!" he was foulmouthed, lewd and obscene.

The magnitude of threat was intense. The army bus driver inflicted fear in us. He robbed us of our professional and humble traits. His violent obnoxious and verbally abusive words left an imprint in my brain. I was on edge and in a loop. I felt as if I was haunted by a nightmare. It was a brutal shock to my nervous system. He revved his bus as he tried to provoke us. A flood of emotions twirled around me like a tornado, as I looked my assailant in the eyes. His eyes were bloodshot red, which triggered a fight or flight response. I was overwhelmed with threat. Guilt circled me like hurricane winds. My heart beat faster… boom, boom, boom, baboom, baboom, baboom, and boom. Faced with a combatant enemy I felt a deeper sense of guilt because my colleagues were carrying me. I blamed myself for placing their lives at risk. They were also threatened by a conspiracy theory. His voice was like a raging fire, which destroyed my confidence. My heart sunk like burning embers. We could not fight fire with fire.

Foul language excited his mouth like flames from a dragon. I was a humble doctor and not a flamethrower. I did not retaliate. His mouth was his devastating weapon. Foul language flew out of his mouth like bullets. I felt like using a fire extinguisher to exterminate his obscene words. I remained passive and calm, to avoid confrontation. He was a glorified radical.

The bus sped off in high speed leaving behind a smoke of dust. My loyal friends carried me for 3km and discovered a military hospital. The army hospital denied access to my colleagues. They asked them to walk back.

I was only 34 years old, a doctor of four years. Men my age were having fun with their family and friends. However, I gave up my life with my wife, child and extended family, to treat patients injured in the war. I was a selfless and altruistic doctor. The welfare of others was an inherent part of my life, as a professional doctor. Dedicating my time to treating my patients was a key dimension, as a doctor. My core value was saving lives, during the war. Working in the war zone, I encountered patients with severe injuries. I worked to alleviate pain and suffering. My altruistic nature intrinsically motivated me to relieve patients of suffering. I did not see my wife and child for nine months. Altruism was inherent in my nature. I refused to take time off from my routine work because my patients entered the hospital by the dozens, with critical war injuries. Altruism was my virtue and deed. While they gave me the saline IV, I thought about the conversation I had with my parents and wife.

"You cannot work or stay at the hospital. It is too dangerous for you," my mother panicked.

"Listen to your mother. It is way too dangerous for you. What's wrong with you," my father was angry.

"Then I will leave you. You will not see your baby again," my wife cried, as if she had separation anxiety.

"You do not understand. I am a doctor. Our Tamil civilians are dying because the army is killing them. They need me. Please understand," my altruistic nature surfaced.

"We may not see you again, if the army kills you," my wife sobbed hysterically.

"I am a government doctor at a government hospital. The army cannot attack the doctors," I assured her.

"No ,no, no!" my family chorused.

"I have to help. I will not listen. I have to treat patients," the stubborn side in me surfaced.

When I said goodbye to them my baby was only three months old. I bid my little girl farewell, before I left. I was badly injured and captured by the army. My family would not know my location. I thought that I was going to die, without their knowledge. They were right. I was on a dangerous mission. My mind jetted back to my capture and I focused on my hunger pangs.

"I am angry, sorry hungry," I shuttered.

"We do not serve food here," the officer's voice echoed through the air like a siren.

"Please sir, I am so thirsty. May I have some tea?" I cried desperately.

"I told you, no. We spoke to officers high up in the military office. They asked us to keep you here for an hour," I detected danger.

"Ok," I was paralyzed with pain.

"You will be going to Anuradhapura with our army vehicle," he displayed an imperative mood.

They placed me in an army vehicle. Despite my chronic pain and severe wounds, the journey in the army vehicle was reckless. The army vehicle bounced like a bouncy ball. The vehicle had no shock absorbers or struts. I feared the unstable ride, as it was incredibly uncomfortable. There was no suspension. We arrived at an army check point, where they meticulously scanned the passengers. They separated the LTTE from the civilians, as if they were sifting flour.

I was in chronic pain. I perspired profusely. I felt hyperglycaemic. I begged for water like a child begging for attention. The army officer called a higher commander to request permission, to give me water. They gave me one and a half litre of water in a coke bottle. I gobbled the water, ingesting it like a wild animal. The water made me perspire and increase my pain. My body told me that something was drastically wrong. My head spun like a top. My nerve signals kept firing, as my wounds turned on the pain sensors. I fell on the grass, as the army continued to scan people. I woke up and asked the army officials for permission to sleep on the grass. They directed me into the waiting bus. I lost consciousness. The notion of the environmental stimuli and self-awareness was absent.

The bus took me to another hospital in an IDP camp, in Vavuniya. I felt like a parcel delivered by a courier company. The IDP stood for Internally Displaced Persons, who were kept at these camps against their will. The camp harboured Tamil civilians from the north east territory, who were displaced during the war. Other civilians were sent to the army hospital. I felt as if I was in a military hostage situation, because the army officer called his superior to discuss my fate. I knew they were talking about me using codes and ciphers, as part of their military and diplomatic ritual. I listened attentively to try to decipher and encipher their confidential encoding. The distinction was as fuzzy as my mind. I wished that I had the key to open up their tactical data. If only I had an algorithm to decipher their message, I would know if they wanted to kill me or save my life. The enemy kept me in the dark, both cognitively and physically. At about 6:30 pm they covered the army truck with a tarp, which was another part of their conspiracy theory and spy code. It was a slithering, sly, scheme shown by the military. They undressed me top up and placed me on a hard, long wooden bench, in the covered bus. The essence of such a secretive plan further tormented me. I felt like an outer space alien, who was not familiar with the modus operandi, of selfish human beings. It was a violation to my basic human rights, not to be given immediate surgery. Instinct told me that I was in danger.

Instinctively, my head turned sharply, and my eyes zoomed in, to the bench opposite to me. It was a hair trigger moment, when I felt fear with telepathy. I was spooked. I saw sheer terror and torment in their eyes. There was non-verbal communication between us. All our bodies reacted to the same sense of fear. We were indiscriminately hopeful. In front of me were three young LTTE girls. As a doctor in the war zone my altruistic nature stepped in and I felt empathy for them. During the armed conflict, I witnessed sexual violence and gang rape by military combats. Rape and sexual assault against young girls and babies were part of the army's occupation. I treated many rape cases at the hospital. Rape became a symbol of a psychological military operation. It was intentionally done to humiliate the opposition. Rape and massacre, of thousands of Tamil civilians, was part of the genocide. It was ethnic cleansing against Tamil civilians. They were raped at gunpoint.

Like a Hollywood movie, the horrific images, endured by the three LTTE girls filtered through my mind. I wanted to fight for justice of these three young girls and give them restitution. I strongly condoned sexual violence in ethnic conflict. I thought about my baby daughter. I could not imagine such an atrocity committed on her or my young wife.

It was a still dark, devastating, dreadful night. The bus came to a sudden halt. I could not figure out the strategy and brutal tactics of the army. They took the three LTTE girls out first, to an army camp that was initially used by the LTTE office. I watched the three girls walk out of the bus bent like candy canes. The rationale and motive flashed through my intellectual mind. I pledged to myself that someday, if I was set free, I would address sexual violence against women and children with the United Nations and other humanitarian organizations. The three LTTE girls were in my thought and prayers. The tactics of the perpetrators were obliquely obvious.

The three LTTE girls blended in with the darkness and demonic chaos. Darkness captivated their spirit and soul. Gloom and destruction followed them, as they encompassed darkness. In their mother's womb they were surrounded by darkness. Darkness eliminated transparency and veiled the three girls in evil. I prayed that salvation would deliver light to them. Darkness was the curtain that hid them from the spiritual light. As they sank deeper into darkness, through prayer, I bestow upon them the light of protection.

The army commander threw me onto the floor of a dark corridor, in the building. He was highly intoxicated. He delivered food to me. The corridor became my new home. The sound of music filled the corridor as I sunk onto the dark, cold floor. I wondered if the music camouflaged the horrific sounds of physical abuse and rape.

The luminosity of morning emerged with the first sight of light. I heard the sweet voices of the LTTE girls, which was a shining light. It bestowed happiness upon me, knowing that they were alive. It was May 16, 2009, a day of reckoning. The military officer took me to wash. I peered through the little window. Horror stabbed me in my chest. That inner vision of death and darkness surfaced. The conflict was simmering, yet rape was broiling. Images of gratuitous pain and aggressive cannibalism jogged through my mind. On the tree in front of the window, sprawled across the branches were the clothing of the three LTTE girls. Instinct told me that they were undressed and raped. They must have been in their early twenties. That was the worse than human trafficking. I wondered how such young girls could resist such brutal military men, with guns. Anger raged through my mind. The corrosive action of rape is a stigma that destroys the victim. Shelling, bombing and shooting were not as destructive as rape. I worried about the three girls, who had no protection against the brutal army officers. It was crime against humanity, in such aggression. I endured their horrific pain, in my grim mind. I could only predict their brutal deaths.

The next day they blindfolded me and shovelled me into a bus.

"Sit down," an army officer's voice retorted.

"Be careful, he may escape," another commanded.

"Sit down," it was a martinet's command.

"Get off the bus," the officer yelled as if commanding an army.

"Why are you taking him off?" another officer sounded confused.

"The order arrived to put him in the cell," his voice was uncouth and raw.

The army officers spoke in Sinhala all the time. It was a native language spoken by the Sinhalese ethnic group in Sri Lanka. I understood the language. I was still blindfolded as they directed me through, a maze of death. They threw me into a small cage made with wire and steel. I felt like a trapped stray animal.

"Why are you locking me up?" my cries were humble.

"The order came, to lock you up," his voice was authoritative.

"When will you take me to the hospital?" I was on the brink of death.

"The commander needs to come and give us orders," he was following his protocol.

"But I need surgery, sir," I knew they showed apathy.

"Commander needs to come!" his tone was apathetic.

"When is he coming," I was calm.

"We do not know," the officer was exclusive.

Each day I asked the same questions, but with no avail. I experienced chronic pain. I had no clean dressing. My wound was septic. A sense of malaise set in and I had a mild-fever. I was a doctor in need of a doctor. A green, foul smelling fluid from my wound needed drainage. They refused to take me to the hospital. My lungs filled with a litre of blood. Each time I moved, my lungs continued to fill with blood. I experienced difficulty in breathing. It was a pulmonary edema and lung congestion. My body struggled with oxygen. I experienced shortness of breath while lying down. Each time I moved blood filled my lungs, and it could not expand. Septic fever set in. Death and darkness stood at my doorstep. No proper antibiotics or painkillers were available to me. I was afraid of permanent damage. The luxury of all medical treatment was not available to me.

Although I was served with food, it was uncomfortable to eat. If I drank it, it caused perspiration, which resulted in more pain. I was a right-handed person, yet my right hand was paralyzed. I had to eat with my left hand. I could not control intake of food with my left hand. Most of the food fell to the ground. I was like a child learning to eat food for the first time. To add to the dilemma, I had unwanted guests for lunch and dinner. It was always a communal meal. It was like a Thanksgiving dinner. My uninvited guests were ants, who shared my food. They merrily enjoyed my meal.

"Please sir, I need urgent treatment," I humbly pleaded.

"We have no power. We are soldiers," they did not care.

"Please, urgent need of surgery," it showed in my eyes.

"You went to a government university to get a medical degree. The government educated you. You turned your back on the government," they were blunt.

"What did I do sir?" tears filled my eyes.

"You gave information to the media. Why did you give information to the media?" he was uncouth and rude.

"What information sir?" I was naive.

"You told the media how many Tamil civilians were wounded in the war. You told the media you have no food and medication," he was angry.

"But I only spoke the truth sir," I continued to be naive.

"Truth, truth… you idiot. Only the Sri Lankan government knows the truth. You are only allowed to talk when the government tells you what to say. Get me… Get me," he was ultimately brain washed and rude.

"Sorry sir," I pleaded.

"We are going to kill you… kill you… yes kill you," he brutally threatened me.

My life was in jeopardy. I was vulnerable. I continued to suffer in my cell for another long week. The army was angry with me. At the hospitals my colleagues joked about the white van and the 4th floor. It was a torture dungeon for all political prisoners, in Vavuniya.

I later discovered that my wife filed a missing person's report. Nobody knew where I was. My wife called several hospitals and she visited the mortuary and looked for my dead body. My family visited the Red Cross, United Nations and other organizations in search for me, but with no avail. It was as if I disappeared off the radar.

I lost a lot of weight. My clothes did not fit me. I was transferred to Vavuniya police station.

"Please take me to Vavuniya hospital," I begged.

"No, we are taking you to the head office," they informed me.

"Where is the head office?" I was curious.

"A place where you belong," they were abrupt.

"With hard-core prisoners," another was sarcastic.

"You are an LTTE," one yelled.

"An LTTE needs to be killed," they chorused.

"Sir, I am a doctor. I save lives," I corrected them.

"You are a LTTE mole," another military officer tried to force his definition of me, on me.

Nevertheless, they gave me a change of clothing. I was allowed to shave. My destiny was unknown, as I was treated like a common prisoner.

CHAPTER 5

The 4th Floor

Everyone feared the 4th floor of the CID. It was a Criminal Investigation Department, where torture was conducted. Aggressive torture was conducted on anyone suspected to be part of the LTTE. (Liberation Tigers of Tamil Eelam). A white van transported political prisoners to the CID's 4th floor. All torture began in the infamous white van. Violent beating, electric wire whipping, pipe beating, and suffocation were part of the modus operandi of the officers on the 4th floor. All interrogation took place, once the suspect was stripped naked. Women were sexually abused and treated as domestic slaves. Metal rods and batons were used to beat them by uniformed army officials. Anyone who betrayed the government was sent to a dilapidated, dark dungeon room on the 4th floor. They were branded with cigarettes and maliciously beaten. Males and females were raped at gunpoint. Metal rods were used too scorch political prisoners. Steel toed boots were used to inflict pain, by kicking. All the political prisoners on the 4th floor, were accused of being part of the LTTE, without factual evidence. Some prisoners, who hung upside down, were submerged in water, then asphyxiated.

Police officers arrived in Vavuniya to transport me to Colombo, in a police jeep. The trip took about four hours. To me, the trip seemed like days because of my chronic pain. The pain spoke to me. It was obvious that the prolonged pain told me that something more serious existed. The physical pain took a toll on my mental health as well. My brain sent signals through severe pain. The pain was sore, stiff, stinging, squeezing, shooting and throbbing throughout my body. The pain made me depressed. In addition, to the pain, I had a deep premonition of imminent danger. I had a hunch that they were going to deliver me to the 4th floor in Colombo. I had an inner dialogue with myself. I was a professional doctor who saved lives. I had to convince and console myself, to deal with grief. In a time of deep, disastrous, distress, I sought solace in engaging with an inner dialogue.

The police officers manoeuvred me out of the jeep as if it was part of their military training. I knew that they were going to manoeuvre my mind to betray my soul. It was early parts of the morning and I was thrown into darkness, with evasive movements. I was surrounded by the sound of silence. I greeted darkness with fear. I did not have the physical strength to conquer my fear. The combination of silence and darkness was threatening. I felt isolated surrounded by darkness and silence. The only company that I had were my thoughts. Silence embraced my thoughts. The realm of silence threw me into a state of panic. Noise at the hospital occupied my mind. The brutal screams and howling cries at the hospital distracted my thoughts, and I embraced my identity. I evoked my sense of sound hoping to hear some noise, as silence surrounded me. Exploring silence brought me to fear. I surrendered hopelessly to the stillness of silence and the darkness of the night. Silence foreshadowed death. I had no weapon to combat silence. I found myself in a state of sedate phobia. I felt a panic attack. It was the calm before the storm. Brutal torment etched itself in my mind. I associated silence with the dead. I feared that the silence would break with an amplified military command. Silence introduced me to a lack of civilization, which brought me inherent anxiety.

The police officers directed me to an old jail building, which resembled a haunted house.

A different phobia set in. I expected devilish blood sucking vampires to carry me in. It was spooky and I was spooked. I wondered who introduced Halloween night to Colombo. Physiologically, my body responded with excessive perspiration. I went into fight or flight mode.

I ingested a powerful concoction of trauma, fear, agitation and torment. My mind sent me a chemical message.

I expected to meet death. I was overwhelmed with anxiety. My thoughts were in chaos. As my heart and muscles contracted, my breathing was rapid. I sharpened my vision in the darkness. I expected the doors of the jail to fly open. I imagined a black raven fluttering its wings rapidly. I expected to see bright lights which read, "A Doctor who Testified Genocide." My pupils dilated as I perceived danger.

"Walk straight and into the elevator," the officers harsh words broke the silence.

"Yes sir," my heart pumped more blood.

"In," he yelled as if it was a physical threat.

"Yes," I abided by his command.

The ride in the elevator was like a thriller movie and it triggered fear in me. I expected the door to open with a vivid imagery of black bats flying around. As the door opened, my primal fear surfaced. I almost jumped out of my skin. My teeth began to chatter and grind. A lightning bolt jolted through my body. I shook violently and felt as if my soul left my body. I faced fear head on, with goosebumps tingling on my skin. My respiratory rate increased, and I wondered if my breathing would expire. My heart beat was like a tabla, an Indian classical drum. The fingers and palms of my left hand moved to the beat of my heart, as if I was playing the tabla. My heart vibrated in the tabla mode.

"Thakitatham, thakitatham, thakanakatham...," my heart beat violently like a tabla drum and mirudangam mantra.

"Thakitathakitatham, thakitathakitatham…," was the rhythm of my heart.

The elevator door slid open. It evoked my sense of sight. Like a camera lens my eyes focused on the wall opposite to the elevator. I endured the most striking physical and psychological pain, as I ventured out of the elevator in disbelief.

The words written on the wall was what I feared and anticipated. It was like a spooky mantra. It was written in three languages.

4th Floor (English)

4 Maady (Tamil)

4 VeniThadduwa (Sinhala)

Those words stabbed me like a dagger thrust in my chest. The 4th Floor were words that confronted me like a combat. I perceived the ritual and ceremonial torture, which took place on the 4th Floor. Those words were a symbol of death. It symbolized assassination, torture and murder. Those words were so potent that it stripped me of my manhood. I knew that I was defenceless. I was powerless, vulnerable and susceptible to torture. Nevertheless, I was the doctor who testified to genocide, with the foreign news media. I did not expect to be treated like a prisoner.

Silence filled the air. There were no people and no staff present. They explored all measures of treating me like a prisoner. They took away all my belongings, including my clothing and jewellery. A doctor became an inmate. It was a dormitory styled prison. There were also cells for violent inmates, who were high risked prisoners. They stripped me of my dignity as a doctor, when they took my fingerprint. It was so absurd because in Sri Lanka, the professionals signed their names. Those who were illiterate were expected to provide their fingerprints. It was not a biometric identification system to scan fingerprints. It was an ink pad where they rolled my thumb and pasted it on paper.

There were small caged cells where prisoners settled in. A narrow corridor separated the adjacent cells. They placed me in the corridor on a mat. My physical condition was pathological. Parts of my lungs filled with a litre of blood. My inflammation was chronic. I feared that it would lead to a dysfunction in my lungs. I could not sleep, and I was in distress. My condition could be diagnosed as a pulmonary edema, as blood accumulated in my lungs. Hypoxia set in. I could not breathe due to inadequate levels of oxygen in my lungs. The bomb blast was a blunt trauma to my chest and this resulted in penetrating trauma. I was refused intensive care. I was afraid that cyanosis would set in, where my body lacks oxygen. My human rights were violated because I was not given a mechanical ventilation or fluid replacement. An excessive amount of blood to my lungs led to pulmonary edema. My situation was lethal, and death held my fragile hand.

I visually captured the sight of the other doctors who worked with me. My instinct told me that they planned to kill me. The next morning, they delivered tea to me in a coke bottle. I was captured and in jail for nine days without treatment. The government had vented feeling of anger towards me. The other doctors cried when they saw me because I was in severe need of intensive care.

At about 10pm, they transferred me to the Colombo National Hospital. I shed 23 kilos. They tried to handcuff me, when my right hand was paralyzed. I was treated harshly, like a prisoner. Hemothorax set in, as I had difficulty breathing. They were aware that I was a government doctor and a director of the district. The shrapnel of the bomb hit me on May 15, 2009. Ten days expired, and I was sent to the hospital for treatment. The doctors at the hospital knew that I was in dire straits. They could not believe that I was treated as a prisoner. After an x-ray and intake of antibiotics, I was sent to a ward with several beds. Two police officers watched over me, as if I was a common criminal.

I looked around at the other beds. There were hardcore criminals handcuffed to the beds. Those lucrative criminals were inherent thugs, violent hard-core drug dealers, rapists, murders, serial killers and distinct classification of dangerous criminals. The criminals were all of Sinhalese decent.

The officer coiled the palm of his hands around his mouth as if it was a bugle or trumpet. He made a loud trumpet sound as if announcing a schedule or important message. The trumpet call gained all the criminals' attention. The overtone of the sound brought silence into the ward and the Sinhalese criminals glared aimlessly at the officer. The trumpet call signalled attention.

"I would like to announce to all of you that you have a very important friend joining you today," the officer had a cynical attitude as he pointed his finger at me.

"To join all of you in this ward today we have a Liberation Tiger of Tamil Eelam, LTTE," he smirked.

"We will beat him, kill him," the Sinhalese criminals gave a drum roll.

They all looked at me like a pack of hyenas. They giggled at a high-pitched voice. They clenched their teeth together and began to grind them. I could hear the chatter of teeth. In between the grinding of teeth, they began to growl like bears. To make matters worse, they all had crooked teeth. They clenched their teeth as if they wanted to attack me. The one closer to my bed gnashed his teeth hard. I was petrified.

"I will kill you," one gave me a blurring glare.

"I murdered many LTTE people," another's face morphed.

"I will kill you he, he hehee!" his eyes were demonic.

"I will tear up your skin," a twisted face yelled pounding his handcuffs on the metal bed.

"Let's kill this LTTE mole," another had a demonic possession, as if he stepped out from the legend of the demons.

I encountered a world of ruthless creatures. I could not focus on their faces because their expression scared me. They gave me a cold shattering chill. They were not human beings. They were on the verge of attacking me, like monsters. Their eyes were dark and powerful. Their crazy eyes were full of rage and evil. I felt as if I was in a paranormal world. Negative energy surrounded me and I was paralyzed with fear. I shook as if having a seizure, surrounded by psychopaths. I encountered peculiar reactions from adult men. A dark cloud hovered above them. The clenching of their teeth rituals continued, as if they were possessed by a demon. Disembodied evil creatures surrounded me. It colored my world with fifty shades of black. I was in a demonic realm. I loathed their presence. Their blood curling laughter felt like paranormal activity. One buzzed like a mosquito, as he glanced at me, in a trance like state. They all had evil eyes, as if they could conjure up magic, to destroy me. A premonition told me that they would kill me.

The janitors further instigated the situation. They made conscious attempts to vicariously intimidate me.

Even the doctor orchestrated bullying. He spoke in Sinhala, not knowing I understood the language.

"We gave him food on a dirty plate," a cleaning staff derived enjoyment from watching others laugh.

"He is sad because his LTTE leader died," the doctor treating me gossiped in Sinhala.

"The LTTE leader is his boss," a junior doctor laughed.

"He should have died too," the doctor gossiped unprofessionally, in Sinhala.

The junior doctor, janitor staff and other patients gossiped about me, in Sinhala. Malicious gossip entertained them but humiliated me. They painted a picture of me as an undesirable character. The mocking was based on discriminatory factors. I was targeted based on cultural discrimination. I was the only Tamil civilian or prisoner in the ward. I was not treated with dignity according to ethical and moral standards. The junior doctor derived pleasure from humiliating me because of his own cultural biasness. Being in the position of power was a tactic to enforce others to bully me too. I was demeaned and targeted.

After ten days of chronic pain, I was taken to the operating theatre for surgery. The operating theatre was intimidating yet the doctor was very professional. The Cardiac Unit was illuminated with lights, which illuminated my spirit. The doctor respected me as a bona fide doctor and inevitably treated me with respect. After surgery he bestowed upon me the honour of using the Doctor's lounge. I revelled at the notion of being treated as a patient and a doctor. In that context all I wanted was to be treated with respect and given my human rights.

I embarked on the pursuit of happiness, when I discovered that four of my doctor friends were in the same hospital. My clothing did not fit me, so the four doctors bought me clothing. However, the general rhetoric was that they were not allowed to see me, according to police orders. The real world unfolded in front of me, when those doctors conveyed their love to me. I gained back my prestigious position as a professional doctor, knowing that my friends were close by. My self-esteem returned. I felt as if I was placed on the rating polls. Food, fruit and slippers were also sent to me. Knowing that friends were around reinstated my self-confidence.

That night hell broke loose. After surgery I needed time to relax, recuperate and heal. I endured several hours of interrogation from the officers. The interrogation was brutal, cruel and forceful. They challenged my knowledge on working at the hospital. Their interrogation technique involved forcing me to confess that I treated the LTTE members at the hospital I worked at. The interrogation agent provided different scenarios, to force me to reveal that I was an LTTE member. I denied such accusations. There was no moral justification to prove the agent's point. Every Tamil civilian was a suspect, of being part of the LTTE. My confession was brutally honest. I was guilty of treating Tamil civilians injured by shelling and bombs.

"So, you are a big man with the LTTE?" he was ready to collect information, by putting words into my mouth.

"No Sir," I pleaded.

"All Tamil doctors support the LTTE," he retorted.

"No Sir," I was sleep deprived.

"We have proof that you were part of the LTTE," he inhibited my ability to express the truth.

"No Sir," he prevented me from expressing the truth.

"You gave medicine to the LTTE?" he engaged in deception disregarding my views.

"No Sir, I did not," I confronted the truth.

"Now tell me the truth," his anger was like an earthquake, ten on the Richter scale.

"Sir I worked for the government, not the LTTE," I exposed the truth, yet he looked at me as a liar.

"What connection do you have with the LTTE," he did not let me sleep.

"I am a government doctor, Sir," I was exhausted as he interrogated me for about four hours.

"I will torture you...you hear me," he assassinated my character.

"I am speaking the truth," he used mental torture to elicit information, while violating my rights.

"Why are you in a War Zone?" I experienced contorted stress and distress.

"I have altruistic qualities. I am a doctor who cares for civilians and my people," he continued to needle me.

"What is that... what do you mean altruistic?" it was obvious that such a positive word was not part of his vocabulary.

"I am a selfless doctor...I care for the injured people. I sacrificed my life with my family and friends to care for injured people sir," he did not believe in the traditional virtue, which was core to my personality.

"You are a liar...dirty liar," he did not believe in the rights to enhance welfare, without reciprocity.

"I worked with the Sri Lankan government approval. I ran a government hospital, Sir," he played a bleak buzzing, blunt music, which exhausted my cognitive functioning.

"You are a political prisoner. You belong to the LTTE. We will kill you," the validity of his arguments was irrelevant and obnoxious.

"I did not do anything illegal, sir!" four hours of interrogation drained all my energy. Sleep called my name.

They transported me back to the 4th Floor. I had an appointment for a nerve graft in ten days. A segment of my nerve needed replacement. My injured nerve needed to be bridged by a graft. They planned to perform another surgical procedure after two weeks. They sent me into a second interrogation and torture chamber. They violated all international laws of human rights.

"Why did you work in a war zone?" it was like a scratched record.

"I am a government doctor, sir," he tried to generate a negative response from me, which was beneficial to him.

"What part did you play in the LTTE?" he threatened me with his bombastic voice.

"I was a government doctor," they did explicit research on me.

"Your surgery has been postponed for three months," those words elicited fear in me.

"Why?" I knew that it was part of my mental torture.

"We do not know but it is postponed for three months," I was surprised, shocked, scared and devastated.

"Why am I in prison? I do not understand sir?" I sounded naive.

"Do you not hear what I said," the commander was furious.

"Your release depends on the Sri Lankan president and his brother," they wanted to elicit false confessions by brainwashing me.

I rode the moral horse. I refused to give any false confessions. I later discovered that my three doctor colleagues conspired to give false information, prior to their interrogation session. They discussed that if they played naïve, the interrogation would be smooth sailing. They played to the tune of the military commander and provided answers that were pleasing to the government. I was brutally honest, which worked against me. My report differed when contrasted with the other doctors. My response was incompatible and deviated from my doctor colleagues. Such a contradiction put me in a state of conflict.

"According to the terrorist act in Sri Lanka, we can keep you in for one year or more. After the court case you will be sent to jail for five years. Your release depends on the Sri Lankan president and his brother, yet again. The president and his brother are angry with you because you damaged their name with the media. We will keep you in for one year. The president and his bother are very angry with you. If you make them happy then they will release you. There is a press conference, where you have a chance to tell the media what we want you to say. The government wants you to clear their name," he tried to bribe me.

"Your surgery will be postponed until... after the medical conference. You have to agree with the other doctors and the president. You will lose your family, kid, wife, parents and life. We will kill. At the press conference you will recite the words that we tell you to say or... we will kill you. The other doctors agreed to say, what we tell them. The press will ask you questions. We will tell you how to answer the questions. You have to memorize the answers we give you. The government wants you to give the media new figures of war casualties. Remember we will kill you and your family," he tried to bribe me through blackmail.

Like actors all the doctors had to rehearse their roles. I was part of the fake news team. When all five doctors entered into the room, a drum roll played in my mind. The room was filled with a swarm of paparazzi. I felt like a high-profile celebrity. It was lights, camera, and action. Journalists were present from various media outlets, for sensational tabloid news. The flash of the cameras was like a flash of lightening, which illuminated our lives. We were manipulated by cameras. For a second, it reminded me of the flash of the bomb that landed close to me. I felt like I was in a melodramatic, elaborate, exclusive, elevated and glamorous setting of Bollywood.

The cameras seduced me. The flash lights enticed me, with its bright charm. I felt like the allure of Hollywood, which was enchanting and powerful. The setting bewitched me with the dazzle of camera lights. I was mesmerized with its brightness. The presence of the media journalist enthralled me. I was hypnotized to engage in fake news. Nevertheless, I was beguiled by their presence. I spontaneously hoodwinked the media with false answers. Like the magician, I deluded the media with trickery and diverted their attention away from the Tamil genocide in Sri Lanka. A multitude of false answers deceived the media yet protected the Sri Lankan government.

A fake answer was my boarding pass, to check in to reality. My fake news identified me as a passenger of freedom. Fake news and lies provided me with a ticket of departure to see my wife, child, parents, friends, relatives and colleagues. My mind was focused on my scheduled time of departure, which was a ticket out of the 4th floor. I narrated lies to avoid torture. I was excited to check in to the kiosk of freedom.

After the press conference, I received my boarding pass of freedom. They released me. I reunited with my wife after two weeks. It was heart-wrenching to see my wife and baby. My nerves of steel shattered and I broke down and cried like a baby. My tears would have filled a well. My emotions took control over me, as my tears rolled in like a tsunami wave. The marathon of tears looked like a rain storm. I did not visualize that a "hello" was more devastating than a "farewell." I sobbed to my heart's content, with such emotional upheaval. I hugged my wife as if suffering from separation anxiety. Tears welled in my wife's eyes and streamed down her face. Her tears were like a river overflowing its banks. My throat was on fire. I swallowed saliva as if swallowing golf balls. I held her fragile body in my arms and promised her that I would not let her go. My sacrifice was her pain. Bitter emotions twirled around us like a raging tornado. My wife drowned in a pool of emotions. She was in excruciating, emotional sadness.

Lionel Richie's song, "Hello" played through my mind as I reminisced about my lonely days on the 4th floor. It conjured up deep memories of missing my wife. I dwelled upon being solo. I gave her my sacred promise to stay by her side.

My heart melted like candle wax, when my nine-month-old baby was placed in my arms. The meet and greet was so moving. A political prisoner was transformed into a dad. I shook like jelly. I melted like ice cream on a tropical summer's day. She looked me in the eye, with fear. The intimate moment morphed into a battlefield. She kicked and screamed because she did not know me. She was three months old when I left. At nine months I was introduced to her once more. Her instinct alerted her, about the danger of being with a stranger. She developed stranger anxiety and gave a gut-wrenching cry. It was a slow desensitization progress. I cried because I was not there to experience her milestones. She vigorously jumped into the arms of my wife in distress. She grew hysterical, as she glanced at me with curiosity. It aroused deep emotions in me and tears flowed, as I thought about the babies who we lost at the hospital. I constantly thought about my baby, when I treated those babies. I wept aloud. It was a bittersweet moment. My parents were in an IDP camp, so they could not visit me.

My wife applied for me to go to a private hospital for surgery. It elated my spirits because on a Saturday, I was allowed two visitors. I wrote a letter to the Red Cross to see me. Like a postman my wife delivered it to them. Unfortunately, at the private hospital, I encountered the same doctor who postponed my surgery. He was sceptical to perform surgery on me, because he was afraid of the government. The government influence on the health system was controlled.

"Doctor may I please travel to India, London or Canada to get medical treatment," I begged.

"No, you cannot leave the country," he was assertive.

Eventually I received surgery in August 2009, after the media conference. The other doctors were summoned to go to court. The judge visited me in the hospital. He had fear in his eyes like a stray puppy. The judge granted me a one million Sri Lankan rupee bail. It was paid by my wife and brother. I continued to stay at the hospital upon my release.

At the inquiry, the truth surfaced like oil on water. The doctors were recognized for their dedicated service, hard work and sacrifice. However, our release was subjected to the approval of the president of Sri Lanka and his brother, who was at the head of security of defence (2005-2015). After the inquiry the CID officials became friendlier.

My wife stayed at a hotel about 200km from the jail. The military undertook to investigate and follow my wife, while she lived at the hotel. The surveillance on her repeatedly invaded her privacy. It intimidated her because she was alone at the hotel with our baby. They monitored her every move. To add to that chaos, the hotel management were obnoxious and rude. In layman's terms they kicked my wife out of the hotel, in favour of the military. She proceeded to seek shelter with a friend. The C.I.D stalked and harassed her. They constantly monitored her. Eventually out of fear her friends forced her to leave. She cried as they turned her out, because she was with our eight-month-old baby. My wife carried the sorrow in her heart. She carried a baby in her arms, with elated love. She carried my problems like books in a backpack. My problems were heavy, yet she endured the pain. The road was long. She packed tears, sadness, torment, frustration and grief in her backpack, as she left her friend's house. Her friends shed crocodile tears, while luring her out of their house.

The country was still unstable, after the war. Corruption set in. Hatred for Tamil civilians continued to spring. She travelled by taxi with an eight-month baby into the still night. She escaped the wrath of the military. She passed the massacre of Tamil civilians. She drew our baby closer to her chest, to provide her with security and warmth. The threat from the military followed her like a shadow. The roads further on were desolate, intense and hostile. The ruins of what were once homes were vivid. She nursed our baby as she embarked on a dangerous journey, in search of a shelter. The journey was long. She endured the psychological pain, for the sake of the baby. She cuddled the baby as she called upon her guardian angels to deliver her spiritual strength. Her leap of faith depended on her spiritual protection. Her spiritual strength summoned her to be physically strong. The trip was difficult for her and the baby. The government army soldiers were perched on every hill, as she trekked in search of safety. She yearned for a home with family. She took courage to feed her baby to prevent hunger pangs, although her stomach growled with hunger. Her faith was challenged. She embraced the baby with humble thoughts. She was a beacon of strength for her husband and child. The taxi rattled up the hills and rolled down the valley. It was not a stable night because she could hear subtle sounds of gunfire and shelling.

As the sound intensified, she tugged onto her first born, with sentimental thoughts. Her first priority was to cultivate love for a child, in a setting embittered with war. In an impoverished country with so much hatred, she was eager to find shelter for her child. There was a rigorous bang and the taxi came to a sudden halt. She saw the bright light of an angel, who spiritually calmed her down. The vital presence of spiritual angels conveyed protection. She meditated and prayed. She endured faith in God. She wondered if the loud bang meant that the taxi was hijacked by the military. Her Hindu faith was strong, and she hoped that her angels would deliver safety to her baby. If she died with her baby, she prayed that her spiritual angels would deliver her safely to her ancestral community. She longed to be in a temple of purity. She prayed that her husband would escape tyranny and injustice.

She felt as if she was surrounded by a bright blue light of purification. She opened her eyes and there in front of her was a village. It was serendipity. She felt the fortunate stroke of her spiritual angel. By sheer fluke a Christian Orphanage opened their doors and warmly accepted her and her baby. Open arms embraced their presence. The embroiled presence of the military died down like an onset of cancer. She found solace in the Christian Orphanage. She and her baby received the fellowship of love.

Amnesty International celebrated human rights. They played an active role in transporting my wife to the hospital to see me. Members of Amnesty International welcomed me and played a robust part in providing my wife and child with safety. The war was over in May 2009 but there were soaring cases of war crime and human rights abuse. The disappearance of Tamil civilians was rife. Tamil men and women were picked up by the white van. Corruption in the IDP camps continued. Families in foreign countries sent millions of dollars to release their loved ones from the IDP camps. Bribery and corruption set in.

My mind sang a song of sorrow, as tears streamed down my sunken cheeks:

I did not choose to flee,

I was finally set free,

Now a prisoner of my soul,

It's my inner strength they stole,

Forced to refute war crimes,

The brutally of those times,

Allegations against the antagonist,

I now emerge as a protagonist,

Brutally trapped in a war zone,

Listen to that suffering tone,

The Sri Lankan civil war ended,

Yet my broken heart has not mended,

Smothering, stuttering, suffering,

A brutal, bloody form of governing,

Trapped civilians left to die,

A professional doctor left to cry,

The hospital was under attack,

Medicine and food was a lack,

Medicine they refused to send,

Patients' wounds could not mend,

They refused to send any food,

A terrifying and indicative mood,

The hospitals were brutally shelled,

Missiles, the government soldiers propelled,

I live to tell a tale of torment,

And a tale of woe and lament,

Trapped in the bloody killing fields,

Civilians trapped as human shields,

A bloody day on May 15, 2009,

The Tamil civilians saw a decline,

This is my humanitarian analysis,

It leaves me with total paralysis.

CHAPTER 6

Flashback- the war in 2006

In 2006 voting began. The negotiations between the Sri Lankan government and the Liberation Tigers of Tamil Eelam (LTTE), with Norway proved unsuccessful. Both sides feared that either side would manipulate the situation, which would result in war. All Sri Lankans needed peace. The LTTE leader, who was born on 26 November 1954, founded the LTTE, a militant group, who sought an independent state for Tamils in Sri Lanka.

Prabhakaran was not in favour of a war. Mahinda Rajapaksa became the prime minister and the peace talks continued. The Sri Lanka Monitoring Mission (SLMM) was active in April 2006 to monitor a cease fire. A LTTE female suicide bomber attacked an army chief in 2006, who was badly injured. That was the inciting force, which led to war. She was symbolic of a potent weapon in Colombo, the capital of Sri Lanka. The government attacked the eastern province.

Mutur, which was part of the Trincomalee district was attacked because of the harbour. Huge oil tanks were stationed in the harbour. Tamils rejected the Indian governments offer to establish a factory there. The Sri Lankan government attacked the area under false pretence. They attacked the LTTE. Tamil civilians were killed and injured. It was a remote area with about seventy thousand people, depleted of water, electricity, hospitals and phones. The government doctors refused to work there because it was so remote. There were isolated incidents of doctors visiting the area for first aid treatment. The government feared that if the people visited government areas for treatment, it would draw too much of media attention.

In the LTTE controlled areas people were admitted to Eachehilampattu Hospital. Patients were not allowed in the government-controlled area of Batticaloa. Patients died at Eachehilampattu Hospital because of lack of doctors, no medication or proper medical facilities. The hospital only employed one permanent doctor. Doctors were not willing to work there due to lack of restaurants, known as hotels. The army camp was in close vicinity of the hospital. The government derived measures to send rotating doctors to the hospital. My friend from the Public Health staff provided me with relevant facts about the hospital. He furnished me with information about the suffering of patients due to the lack of a professional doctor. During that period of time Muslim and Sinhalese people occupied the Ampara area.

Immediately, I was ridden with guilt. Moral and ethical principles hammered at my brains, as if talking to me. Freud's psychoanalytic theory of the id, ego and superego confronted me, like gang warfare. My inner spiritual nature surfaced like a lotus flower. The image of all the Hindu deities flashed in front of me. My body transposed into a sacred dimension.

Altruism slapped me across the face. Virtue danced around me like a classical Bharathanatyam dancer. The Hindu philosophy of Sanathana Dharma shook my hand. It reminded me to treat everyone equally. The Hindu philosophy of Vasudaiva Kutumbakam, challenged me to include all people in this Universe as part of my extended family. That is when I became a selfless person. Altruism flowed through my veins like blood. Altruisms enhanced my happiness. I sacrificed my life, for the wellbeing of others. I expected no rewards from others. My gratification emerged, when I saw others in perfect health. Loyalty became my middle name. Altruism became my last name. My heart turned into a Temple, reserved for spiritual rituals and love for all. The ambiance of spiritual knowledge embraced my soul. I reflected on divinity and my inner soul. Divine love blossomed in me like a lotus flower. I inhaled a sense of spiritual fragrance and exhaled a sense of satisfaction. My patients elevated my spirit, and I illuminated their lives. Every breath I took in, came with a high vibration and spiritual charm.

The government hospitals provided free treatment. The wait was short. Doctors engaged in treating the actual problem. I was so happy in Amparai because of its peaceful nature. My wife worked close by as a teacher. I worked there for one and a half months before the war began. It was a friendly and small community of Muslim people. Against the wishes of my wife and family, I transferred to a risky LTTE controlled area of Eachehilampattu, at my own will.

There, I met the Health director. There was no running water. They had one generator that provided electricity for one hour. We needed fire wood for cooking and candle light for electricity. It was scorching hot. My altruistic nature set in therefore, I had no need to complain. I was content with my little doctor's quarters, which became my home. My bathroom was a nearby well. I was offered a hospital ambulance to go home each night. However, I chose to stay at the hospital, to develop the hospital. In the ambulance they offered me, I sent seriously ill patients to Batticaloa and Trincomalee, to get better treatment.

I requested to use a generator from 6pm to 10pm for emergency purposes. The Red Cross was kind enough to increase the water supply. I introduced an in-patient treatment at the hospital. A maternity ward commenced, with my initiation. I pioneered a beautiful and exotic landscape around the hospital. The hospital was like a lotus flower. It emerged from musky waters, into an exotic place. Like a lotus flower purity and beauty surfaced. During the day the hospital blossomed like a lotus. The hospital was a symbol of rebirth.

Each morning the sun stretched its arms around the building, as if giving it a spiritual hug. At night the moon shone, illuminating the building, which stood still like a spiritual angel. The Eachehilampattu hospital was resurrected into a statue of liberty. It bonded me with my patients. At that stage I was a 31-year-old doctor. I cleaned the hospital so that purity and spirituality walked through the doors. I introduced spiritual enlightenment to a once ancient ruin.

With embedded wisdom, intelligence, knowledge and empowerment, I transformed Eachehilampattu Hospital into my lotus flower. Each ward, which I introduced, became a petal of spiritual awakening. The hospital was my symbol of love and compassion. I gained spiritual enlightening by thoroughly cleansing the hospital and bringing it to life. Lakshmi the Hindu goddess of prosperity walked through my hospital doors.

I was also symbolic of the lotus flower. At the age of thirty-one, I resembled a bud. As the years passed, I blossomed into that lotus flower, playing a major role as a medical doctor in the war zone.

At 31 years old, while other people of that age were partying and socializing, I dedicated myself to treating patients. I surpassed happiness and reached bliss. One day, I retired in my doctor's quarters when a dust storm emerged. A gust of loose dirt rolled in like a thunderstorm. Fascinated by the noise and dust cloud, I ran out to explore that natural phenomenon. I blinked my eyes several times. Like a character from a fairy-tale a woman emerged from the dust storm on a three-wheeler motorbike. She had a severe asthma attack and could not breathe. She experienced bronchospasm. The muscles around her airways tightened. I rushed her into the hospital ward. Her respiration stopped, and she collapsed on the bed. As a new doctor, I launched into reality. I had to compromise my theory for practise. My scientific knowledge transposed into sincere practise. I treated her with haste. Her heart rate reduced, when I checked her pulse. To add to the commotion, my staff had no practical knowledge on how to operate medical equipment.

"Call the midwife," I instructed.

"She is in the bathroom doctor," they were naïve.

"Get her out, I need immediate help," my voice went off like an ambulance siren.

"Get me a tracheal tube to insert into her trachea," I needed to maintain her airway. They did not know what that was.

"I will help you doctor," the midwife was the only knowledgeable person present, yet she was twenty minutes late.

The patient vomited with the endotracheal tube. Her vomit flew all over me like a shower spraying out water. I began to perspire. The vomit sprayed all over my face and body. I looked like a monster made of slime. I was covered in vomit. Vomit dripped down me like candle wax. She threw up spicy curry and rice all over me.

"Doctor do you want to wash?" the staff could not stand the smell of the vomit.

"No, I do not care about the vomit on me. All I care about is curing her," altruism lived in me.

"Get me the ambulance driver and fast," the haste in my voice showcased urgency.

The fermentation of vomit evoked the sense of smell in those around me. The sour smell made its way all around the hospital, like smoke spreading through a building. It was the fermented smell of curry and rice. Other acidic smell and chemicals from the stomach surfaced. The chemical composition of vomit mixed with fatty acids, made the other staff members puke. When a baby pukes on a mother, the mother does not react, but focuses on the child's medical condition. Likewise, I was that mother and focused my attention on saving the patient. I was not moved by the sight or smell of vomit. She did not evoke my sense of sight, smell, taste or touch. She evoked empathy in me.

By ambulance I transported her to Batticaloa Hospital, with manual ventilation. She was still unconscious. I rode along with her at 7 pm, treating her as we meandered through rough terrains. The ambulance zigzagged. At times like a snake it meandered through serpentine, twisty roads. The dusty roads were intricate, as we wandered vigorously and erratically through the route. Anxiety set in because it was dangerous. We were in the middle of a ruthless civil war. Shelling continued, and the sounds of bombs erupting flawed my emotions. I had to mask my emotions to save my patient. Guilt stalked me. I had to strife through my competitive medical endeavours. Her life was in my hands. I would not anticipate death. I did not allow death to diminish or manipulate my self-esteem.

The shelling and bombing, with its heightened sounds did not provoke me to turn back. I had a mission and my goal was mission accomplished. The contagious emotion of depression could not trigger a response from me. I abandoned all negative emotions, which were overwhelmingly toxic. At about 40 km into our journey, she began to breathe. We reached Batticaloa hospital.

"Doctor she is breathing," the ambulance driver observed.

"Yes, she was so close to death," her condition resided in my memory.

"She died, and you gave her life doctor!" another staff member exclaimed.

"You are a hero doctor!" they chorused as my patient began to walk.

"Everyone come, come, come, the doctor performed a miracle!" they attributed her recovery to magic.

"You are a miracle worker and a saint doctor," they examined all odds of beating death.

"I am not Mother Teresa. She is a strong woman," I acknowledged the patient's spiritual strength.

"Other doctors at our hospital work with fear. You are so rational. This is a rare phenomenon," the crowd clapped.

I continued to be modest and humble, as I was faced with the challenging experience of treating patients, brutally injured by shelling. I had to be competent and confident to help my patients. I took on another challenging task to train the sanitary staff who knew very little about medicine. I burned the midnight oil. I worked at the eleventh hour, to train my sanitary staff with medical knowledge. I trained them how to use an IV and injection. They were all Tamil civilians who craved to learn more. With their help I restructured the Emergency room. The hospital had a "rags to riches" story. I built the hospital from scratch into a fully-fledged operating facility.

Chaos set in when the Maavilaaru River, which supplied the Sinhalese villages with water, was shut. They needed a water supply for their rice plantations and cultivation. The LTTE closed the river for personal transportation and forgot to reopen it. It was close to the LTTE control area. This drew the attention of the government because the Sinhalese villages had no water for their Paddy fields.

Negotiations pursued between the Sri Lankan government and the LTTE to reopen the river gate. The issue escalated into a problem. Human Rights organizations intervened. In August 2006 the LTTE refused to be manipulated. The government called upon military action to forcefully open the gate. That vicinity turned into a battlefield. It became known as the Maavilaaru war. The government killed civilians with heavy artillery. I witnessed the death of the hospital I created. The army attacked the hospital. I cried to see Eachehilampattu Hospital transformed into a ruin. The government army aerial attack destroyed bridges and transportation.

Military victory showcased the ugly side of war. There were thousands of casualty deaths due to vicious shelling. Most of the casualties were Tamil civilians. I witnessed war atrocities and genocide. It was the bloodiest was against Tamil civilians. The Tamil civilian casualties met their fatality when the government army openly fired at them.

The song revealing genocide floods my mind, each time I reflect on the term genocide.

Sri Lankan government the antagonist,

Tamil Civilians were the Protagonist,

Tamil woman and children lost their lives,

The genocide took husbands and wives,

To destroy the entire Tamil group,

And it was a bloody military coup,

Violence against a Tamil ethnic race,

Discrimination is such a disgrace,

Genocide is an international crime,

Sri Lanka during the civil war time,

And shelling as fast as lightening,

For Tamil civilians it was frightening,

The massacre of thousands of Tamils,

Educated people with talented skills,

It is against the Human Rights law,

Genocide is exactly what I saw,

A Tamil doctor who testified,

What he witnessed was genocide,

Violent crime against humanity,

Killing the Tamil race is insanity,

An appeal at the Human Rights convention,

Dear United Nations show us prevention,

And the Tamils they tried to destroy,

Vicious, violent soldiers they employ,

Tamil, torture chamber on the 4th floor,

Rape and beating behind the closed door,

Physical, psychological and metal harm,

And slaughtered like animals on a farm,

So, to bring about group demise,

Therefore, killing Tamils cannot be wise,

Birth prevention and forced sterilization,

An intent to destroy the Tamil nation,

Crimes against humanity and ethnic cleansing,

Prevention of all medication and dispensing,

Tamils faced with horrifying brutality,

The Sri Lankan government's brutal mentality,

Amnesty International and the Red Cross,

Sri Lankan government proved to be the boss,

Today there is still no Sri Lankan peace,

Violence against Tamils is on the increase,

What constitutes genocidal actions?

It's all about the Human Rights reaction,

Tamils deprived of higher education,

The Sri Lankan government's legislation,

A medical doctor who cried genocide,

Thousands of Tamil bodies he identified,

As genocide progressed on the loom,

Tamil civilians met their day of doom!

Tamil casualties suffer hunger pangs,

On the gigantic trees the IV bag hangs,

A doctor who still suffers nightmares,

Today stories of genocide he shares,

It is the doctor's genocidal account,

He witnessed the death toll surmount,

He tells his sad story in poetry and prose,

That's the way his genocidal story goes,

Now let's call upon all Human Rights,

To analyze all that genocide ignites,

My song cannot come to an end,

To all Tamils my sympathy I extend.

CHAPTER 7

A Father's Love

One fiery night I proceed to my quarters. I witnessed a pickup truck speed, as if he was in a NASCAR tournament. He advanced through the symmetrical dirt roads, with a high intensity of speed. He ignored the hospital speed limit, which angered me. I had no words to describe the intensity of his speed and his breech of safety measures. He popped some wheelies, as if I was a judge to declare him a winner. I worried that he may endanger the lives of others. He performed some doughnuts as he showcased his horsepower. His hot wheels created a massive dust storm, as he destroyed every obstacle in his way He tore through a massive dust storm. The blinding dirt engulfed his truck. It casted a brown fog over the hospital. I took precautions by shielding my eyes, with the palm of my hands, as I was shrouded by thick dust. Despite my anger, I monitored him. He obscured his own vision. To add to the drama, he blew his car horn as if signalling for my attention. The sound waves vibrated throughout the area. The amplified sound alerted other staff members too.

"Beep beepbeepbeepbeepbeepbeep!" it created a ring in my ear.

The pickup truck came to a sudden halt. The abrupt halt created a loud screech, as he slammed his foot on the break.

"What's wrong with you? What's the rush?" I retorted.

"I work for the LTTE in their garage as a technical mechanic. Doctor, please don't hold that against me," he cried hysterically.

It was the ugliest man I had ever seen. I could not recognise his features because he was covered in grease. His hair and face were covered in black tar or asphalt. It looked toxic. He looked like breaded chicken because on top of the black grease he was covered with dust. He reminded me of a fried mutton roll. His white eyes were illuminated like a monster from a thriller movie. He was an unimaginable horror monster. He resembled a blood sucking creature, which was ready to deliver a corpse to Hell.

He gave off the foul stench of grease. His ghoulish eyes penetrated my soul. I shivered as I almost jumped out of my skin. I was paralysed with fear, and anxiety. His sharp black pupils stared at me like an evil cat. I expected him to pounce on me like a black panther. I imagined him leaping like a panther ten feet into the air and mauling me to death. I wondered if he was prone to hunting doctors. Like a marathon my imagination ran at length. My imagination took control over my mind with compelling images of death.

"Doctor I was working in the garage when I noticed someone carrying this little boy. He is only eight years old. He carried him in with only a pair of shorts. I carried him here from my mechanical shop. I drove him so fast to the hospital, doctor. Please doctor please, please, please save him. He was bitten by an insect. He is going to die. Save him doctor, save him," his voice was so timid and sincere.

"But an insect bite is not so poisonous," I assured him.

"No doctor in the eastern province we say insect bite," he confused me.

"No sir, doctor, in the eastern province we believe culturally that if we say snakebite, then the poison will kill the person. Please doctor we have to say insect bite. I do not want him to die," he was in a state of panic and overwhelmed with anxiety.

"Relax I will take care of him," I tried to calm him down.

The man cried hysterically as I checked the boy. The boy's blood was already poisoned. I tried to keep him calm, as anxiety causes the blood to flow faster. I administrated antivenin, to counter the snake bite. His condition stabilized. However, the man continued to bawl. He could not restrain himself. He cried uncontrollably. It was a gut-wrenching cry. It disrupted his thinking as his bawling spells escalated. I could not disconnect his water works. His crying indicated that he was in total distress.

"Are you the boy's father?" I inquired.

"No," he continued to bawl as if he was at a funeral.

'Are you a relative?" I was not there to interrogate him.

"No," were the only words in his vocabulary.

"What is your name?" I hunted for answers.

"Lingan, Doctor," his cries turned to hiccups.

"Who is this boy, Lingan?" I was puzzled.

"I was working at my mechanic garage and his father brought him in a hurry. He told me that he had an insect bite. I grabbed the boy and jumped into my van. I rushed him to the hospital to save his life. No, I do not know him or his father," he continued with the hic sound.

The boy stabilized. I asked Lingan to go home. He walked around the hospital deep in thought. He was lost in a maze of his own thoughts. I felt empathy for Lingan because he was so preoccupied in his own world. Worrying wreaked havoc on his life. It was as if he had an internal civil war. He internalized some emotional pain and continued to cry. Lingan's mental health took a toll on him. He was totally distraught. It was a marathon of tears.

"Doctor," he broke the silence.

"Yes," I showed empathy,

"I wish you were here two months ago. Then my daughter would have been alive. I know you would have saved her life doctor," he confessed.

Silence filled the air. Only his sobs could be heard. He continued to narrate his story, as I listened attentively. His story ran through my mind like a horrific Hollywood movie. He narrated his plot with the rising action, climax and denouement. His memoir was thrilling and struck a sad note in me. Like a domino effect, I began to cry listening to his touching tale of a father's deep love for his daughter.

The army continued its artillery shelling on Tamil villages. Intense army shelling escalated. Lingan tended to the injured as conflict erupted. As he projected his altruistic nature, he sustained injuries. The army deployed near their village and launched a heavy mortar attack. Hundreds of Tamils were killed. Lingan was wounded in the belly during the episode of shelling.

The LTTE doctors did a laparotomy on him. It took a tremendous toll on his mental and physical health. After surgery, he was sent home to recuperate. Unfortunately, his wound did not heal. His poor health condition was a difficult problem to describe. He could not leap forward into good health. His problematic belly wound continued to bug him.

On one dark rainy night, his eight-year-old daughter went out to the garden to urinate. She suffered a more catastrophic injury. A slithering snake bit her in the garden.

"Appa, Appa help me!" she screamed.

"What happened," Lingan jumped like a panther.

"A snake bit me" she verbalized her issue.

There was no phone or electricity. It was raining heavily. He rushed her to the LTTE Health Centre as they treated civilians too.

It was a dark long journey. He drove with an Ambulance driver. The rain pounded on the vehicle with force. The thunder storm surge caused extensive flooding. The wind speed was rapid. The eye of the storm focused on the vehicle. Lingan's eyes were focused on his baby girl.

"The bridge is damaged," the driver announced.

"The vehicle is going to get struck on the road," Lingan was in panic mode.

"No, we will be ok," the driver misinterpreted the storm.

The ambulance became submerged in the flood. The water had no discipline. It escaped its usual path and flowed with animation. The ground was saturated. The night was pitch-black. The ambulance could not meander through the flood. The flood impacted the whole area. Lightning befriended them. With each electrostatic discharge of lightening it illuminated their path creating instant light.

The road had no traction. It was slippery, which made the tires spin. The area was dead. The stillness told them that no passerby would provide charitable help for safety. The wheels buried itself deeper into the mud. Like a resting patient, the axle of the chassis lay on the ground, as if relaxing. The driver engaged in throttling up the engine. The spinning wheels were like a hamster on its wheel, with aggressive spinning. The continuous revving only embedded the wheels deeper into the mud.

A flash of lightening illuminated his daughter's face. Lingan kissed his daughter on the forehead and caressed her cheeks. A foamy white saliva flowed out of her mouth like ocean waves. The frothy saliva was light, white and bubbly. The flow of foam was steady. Lingan knew that the foaming froth spelled danger.

Death plagued her. The roaring of thunder and the flash of lightning foreshadowed the shrewdness of death. Lingan was not going to generously hand his daughter over to death. Just the way the government army fought the LTTE, he was prepared to fight death.

He delved deep down into his eternal strength and found the courage to destroy death. His eternal soul gave him the spiritual courage to move ahead.

He caressed his baby in his arms with her head resting on his elbow and her legs resting on his other hand. He could not deal with his open belly wound. Like a sprinter he ran through the rain. The heavy thunder was like the beat of the Indian tabla drums. It was music to his ears. Lingan marched to the beat of his own drums, with courage. His heart beat like the tabla drum, as he ran though the pouring rain.

It was pitch-dark. It was painful and difficult. His marathon was to save the life of his daughter. The muddy roads were intense. It was an obstacle course. He ran through his spiritual dimension. His goal was to reach Eachehilampattu Hospital, to save his daughter's life.

While running, his wound slit open. He placed his pain aside and continued to run as if running to the finishing line. His love-oriented journey intrinsically motivated him to move on. He was conscientious and diligent.

His bleeding wound signalled him to stop. His daunting love for his daughter prompted him to move on. He sacrificed his life for his daughter. His extensive, extreme endeavour set his pace. His medal at the finishing line was his daughter's life. The road was difficult and arduous, but he pressured himself to move on.

He had to walk for 3km to the hospital. Darkness became his enemy. They were locked in total darkness. He ran in the depth of darkness. Darkness embraced him and made his journey even more difficult. The source of darkness declared war on him. His tears were downed by the pouring rain. The darkness received him. Darkness made him a blind man. He and his daughter were drenched in rain. Darkness erased his geographical path. He was woven into the black fabric of darkness. His spiritual soul empowered him to fight darkness. He had to make a rampant decision to move on.

He welcomed each vicious flash of lightening. It illuminated his path and destroyed darkness. Each flash of lightening provided him with hope. Lightening was his GPS, which lit his path and moved him in the right direction. The lightening personified good. The darkness was evil. Lightening became his third spiritual eye. It was a divine power, which helped him find his way. Lightening illuminated his mind with wisdom to move on. He was able to look into the eyes of his daughter, who was his spark of light.

The strike of lightening destroyed his enemy, which was darkness. Darkness was a demonic figure, which was unbearable. Lightening restored brightness in his mind, soul and body. Lightening delivered him the vigour to run forward. It purified his path. Its intention was pure as it provided him with wisdom. The brilliant light brought him mental clarity. His load was heavy, but lightening liberated his path and propelled him forward. Lightening showed him his destination. Lightening destroyed the mortality of darkness.

The rain hit on his face cleansing his tears. He was drenched with rain. He held his daughter as her limp, drenched body hung over his arms, as if manifesting creation. Water cleansed his spirit and soul. He could hear the rain falling. He could smell the freshness of the water. He felt the pain on his body. He was able to touch and taste the drops. The rain evoked all his senses. His emotions were as fluid as the water. His little daughter was once protected by water in her mother's womb. Her father ran with her for miles in the rain cleansing her externally. With the heavy rain he found calm and serenity. It was a fascinating yet frightening experience. He gazed at the raindrops, which energized him to move on.

It was midnight when he arrived at the hospital. The lights were off. There were no doctors or ambulance present. The staff was asleep.

"I love you," he whispered in her ear.

"MmmmmmMmmmm," she gave him a loving smile as if expressing her love for her father.

"Don't go my baby, stay with me," a father's love was sincere and profound.

She glared at him with the expression of love. She opened her mouth ingesting some rain. Their eyes locked. The love between father and daughter were so transparent. Her breathing was shallow. She made her final transition from life to death. She died in the arms of her father. She always asked him for permission, yet he did not give her permission to die. It was difficult for him to say his last goodbye. In death he nurtured her by rocking her body, as if rocking a baby to sleep. He rocked her to and fro, as he sang a song of farewell to his little angel. He rocked her to and fro, as her angelic soul departed to a heavenly realm. A father's love never dies.

"Meet you soon on the other side," he bawled,

All hope died in him, as his daughter died in his arms. Blood oozed out of his belly. His physical pain was not as severe as his emotional pain. He felt vulnerable as his daughter took her last breath of life. That glimmer of hope faded. His daughter was the light of his life. It was as if someone blew off his candle light. The flame in him died. His energy and enthusiasm died with his daughter. He looked up at the weeping sky and took a vow that no other man would lose a child. Lingam was a pillar of strength. He dedicated his life to save lives.

He transposed the spiritual love from his daughter onto the little boy, with the snakebite. Love transcended on a new heavenly plain. Love had no barriers. Love emanated from above and explored the heart of Lingan. He identified with the boy's father, as the fundamental love from his daughter bonded him and the boy. The boy's breathing was a rhythm in his heart.

"Doctor, if you were at this hospital two months ago, I know you would have saved my daughter's life," he cried hysterically.

"I know how much you love your people, with compassion," I acknowledged.

"Stay with him doctor… please stay with him," his love for a stranger's son was profound.

It must have been divine, spiritual love, devoid of any negative qualities. We needed the same selfless love to engross the lives of all Sri Lankans, in a time of brutal civil war. Altruism lived on in the heart of Lingam. The ultimate sense of spiritual love gave him a new sense of hope. To him love was tangible.

I treated multiple people for snake bites, at the hospital. The snakes posed as a risk to human lives. The most dangerous species were in the region. Human fatalities were high, as venomous snakes injected their lethal dose. Ironically, I pondered on the fact about who caused more fatalities, the venomous snake or the government army. It was just food for thought, and a crime relief.

What brought me to tears was not the snake bite but Lingan's story. A year had passed by and I searched for him. His story was engrained in my mind. I found him, and he was still so humble.

He announced to the village, "A V.I.P is here to see me. He is such a humble doctor, to look for me," we hugged as the brotherhood of man.

"Your story touched me," I felt his spiritual touch.

CHAPTER 8

Chaos and Conflict

Casualties flooded into Eachehilampattu Hospital like waves of a Tsunami. Armed conflict escalated between the government army and the LTTE. Shelling did not target legitimate military soldiers. Massive Tamil civilians were subjected to shelling. The antagonistic side of the human nature surfaced, like dead bodies floating in a river. The civil war in Sri Lanka saw the death of all moral and ethical values. Tamil civilians suffered the gravity of violence. Discrimination against the Tamil Sri Lankan's led to genocide. The United

Nations took note of the death toll in Sri Lanka. I took note of the deaths of Tamil civilians at the hospital. I saw legitimate targets of the civil war. The civil war between the Sri Lankan government and the LTTE took a different turn of events. The army purged to eliminate the Tamil civilians by shelling them. It took a toll on the social structure of the Tamil society. Chaos and conflict surrounded Eachehilampattu Hospital, like lions surrounding an elephant calf.

It was heart wrenching to see woman and children perish with shelling wounds. The army encroached upon Tamil villages killing thousands of men, woman and children. My heart froze. Sri Lanka became a frozen country with ultimate hatred.

On one faithful day around 7pm a tractor delivered casualties to the hospital. Loud screams of wounded people were like sirens to the hospital. Loud screams of wounded people were like sirens to my ears. It was disturbing to see casualties stuffed into a road side tractor like cattle. It was an enchanting truck from hell. I cursed God's installation of sight, because the visual sight was from a horror movie. Wounded men and woman banged their heads against each other as they squealed in pain. It was as if they made their way to a slaughter house. They were tightly crammed together, as if in a gas chamber. They were squashed together in an antagonizing and shocking position. Even eggs packed in a carton have more room to move around. They had no breathing room or elbow room. There was no room for doubt, the situation was intense. I had to make room in the hospital for the wounded casualties. There was still room for improvement at the hospital.

I welcomed the patients, opening my arms and heart to them. I had my strategies in place to treat them. I was not overwhelmed by the ghostly sight of casualties. My heart melted like wax from a candle. The presence needed my attention. They were of diverse identities and I treated them with dignity. The medical impact on the injured was crucial, no matter what the catalyst of the conflict was.

The hospital was not a grave, but a place to save. The first patient through the door was a man with an opened skull, exposing his brain. There was a handsome young gentleman named Ravi around 30 years old, who resembled a movie actor. He died of a brain injury, yet he looked like a sleeping prince, from a fairy-tale. I had to tabulate statistics of the living and the dead. The dead was attributed to the army shelling. I could not account for those missing in action.

The Eachehilampattu Hospital was close to a hundred-metre-wide River. The Verukal River had no crossing bridge. To reach Batticaloa, there was no road but a river to cross. Passengers were transported on ferry boats operating on mechanical power. Motor boats were also used as means of transportation. A rope was used, attached at both ends of the river. A siren sounded when the ferry was full, to transport people onto the other side. The ferries operated in a primitive mode for hundreds of years. The Sri Lankan government refused to build a bridge for the Tamils, in the Tamil villages.

During the war the government destroyed all bridges and pathways to prevent mobility. The Tamil civilians' installed sand bags, to cross the river. They also repaired the ferries, which were damaged during the war.

As the fight between the government army and the LTTE escalated, the lives of civilians were jeopardized. People took an imperil risk to move around.

Ravi's father worked for a government office in Batticaloa. A father's pain and anguish surfaced when he discovered that Ravi died of his injuries. The father was persistent in transporting Ravi's body home. The roads were barricaded by the government army.

"Doctor please I need to transport my son, Ravi's body home," his heart-ache and distress was audible.

"This is a remote area with no taxi," my empathy surfaced.

"How about on an ambulance, Doctor," he was burdened with anguish.

"The government would not allow us to transport a dead body on an ambulance sir," I was not a bearer of negative news.

"I tried to get a car from Batticaloa but the army did not allow me to come," he choked with tears.

"I understand," I spoke to him with compassion.

"Will you be able to send Ravi's body to the army stop point," he pleaded, in between sobs.

"It is dangerous with the fighting. I cannot think about any other legal way of transporting the body," I tried to console a depressed and distraught father.

He used his influence and persuasive skills to convince the government to allow him to transport his son's corpse, which intrigued me. The government allocated him one hour to collect Ravi's body. With hast he rented a vehicle and arrived at the hospital.

At that crucial moment there was an aerial attack on the ferries. It was sheer catastrophe as the ferries were damaged. The calamity was crippling. It wreaked a havoc on the village.

Ravi's father clasped his hand in prayer and fell at my feet, begging me to transport the body to the ferry. Two days had passed, and the body was in the process of decomposition. It was overwhelming that he did not have a coffin to transport the body.

The indiscriminate shelling continued. They targeted civilians and civilian infrastructure. Missiles and mortar shelling continued to devastate the village. It emerged as a story of an ambulance driver, a doctor, a father and a dead body. I resonated with the father. I was in tune with his deep feeling of distress; my energy field was sincere and pure. Like a magnet, I was able to draw upon the grief of the father. I had a heighted sense of empathy. I ignited my soul, to propel me to help a grieving human being. I found myself in a white bubble of love. My intuition was my guide. My higher self was my master. My heart was my shield. My angels provided me with divine protection. Synchronicity followed me like a shadow. My positive energy propelled me along. My auric field was clear. I chose the path of ascension, to deliver Ravi's body to the other side. My inner strength and higher shield intrinsically motivated me to move forward. I manipulated my own power, to empower me to move forward. The vicious army had no power to weaken my soul, by introducing me to fear.

We made a 3km journey from the hospital to the ferry boat. There was a small fishing boat waiting to transport the father with Ravi's body.

"Thank you, thank you, thank you doctor," Ravi's father fell at my feet as a sign of respect.

"Go safely to your destination" I bid him farewell.

"Doctor how can I thank you. You are so kind," he hugged me and sobbed hysterically.

It was an emotional moment. The father got a coffin and placed it in the fishing boat. As we hugged and bid farewell, the shelling continued. Shells flew over us like a rainbow.

When Ravi's body was still, it was good. As he moved, his body fluids and blood oozed out of the body, creating a decomposing, offensive smell. Some staff members developed a feeling of nausea. The biliousness made them vomit. Some fainted with the queasiness. I bounded Ravi's body with gauze, despite the smell. I treated him as if he was a family member, giving him his last rites. I risked my life to deliver Ravi's body to the fishing boat. It was done on compassionate grounds. The grieving father touched my heart.

Ravi's death was not a mystery. A group of people in Muthur, was mainly Muslims. Muthur was a region controlled by the army. When the war started, the LTTE captured the area. The government army invaded and struck the residential sector. There were two ambulances stationed in Muthur (Trincomalee). Those attacked resorted in using the ambulance to escape. They were Sinhalese, Muslim and Tamil staff members. The Sinhalese feared the LTTE. The staff used the two ambulances to flee from Trincomalee. Ravi was a staff member at the court. He was Tamil.

The two ambulances made their journey though mountainous, desolate areas. They were in fundamental danger. It was a threatening situation, yet an opportunity to escape the shelling. The potential consequence was to ensure protection. Sustaining safety depended on the location of the army.

The army stalked the ambulance as they approached. The ambulance proceeded with ultimate caution. The army suspected that the ambulance was used by the LTTE, since they took control over the region.

"STOP! STOP! STOP!" the army soldier yelled, with an empirical tone.

Out of fear both ambulances sped to avoid conflict. Arjuna drove the first ambulance. The second ambulance driver was Ganesh. They perceived the situation to be a threat. They went into flight mode, as they were triggered by fear. The only word in their minds was survival. Fear cascaded down their spines like a waterfall. The intensity of their fear was massive. Anxiety, anger, aggression and fear marched in front of them like an army. The implication of the situation was tense.

"STOP! STOP! STOP!" the army commanded in Sinhalese, as they fired aggressively into the air.

Their commands triggered mental and physical fear in Arjuna and Ganesh. They faced utmost danger. They could not mobilize the situation. The passengers in the ambulance froze with fear. They were in a difficult position, as they were in the army's spotlight. The word STOP validated danger. They invested in a journey to safety. The mortal enemy surrounded them. They were bombarded with gun shots, on a bumpy track. Ganesh and Arjuna dismissed the stop signs and sped off like a prey escaping capture. The perpetrator was close. Both Ganesh and Arjuna were Tamils, yet they had to respond in Sinhalese to create a shield of protection.

"STOP! STOP! STOP!" the army used a bullhorn.

"Please don't fire, please don't fire," Arjuna responded in Sinhalese.

It was potentially lethal situation. The army gave pursuit. The army perceived them as the enemy. They fired in a hostile and combative manner. It was a case of revenge and intimidation. The violent attack injured the ambulance driver Arjuna. It was a chilling attack. The impact of the shot cracked his skull, exposing his brain. It was appalling how merciless the army was. The ambulance was targeted and Arjuna's wife who was sitting next to him was shot to death. The ambulance came to a sudden halt on a rock. The passengers broke the ambulance window and escaped on foot. The frightening sounds of shelling rang over their heads. They were injured by broken glass.

Ganesh on the other hand directed his hand out of the window, to stop the gunfire. Like a projectile the bullet penetrated the palm of his hand. Some passengers in the ambulance surrendered to the army. Others went to Muthur in search of the LTTE. Those who surrendered to the army were transported to my hospital.

Arjuna was Tamil. His last words were in Sinhala, when he pleaded to the army to stop firing. When he arrived at the hospital he continued to speak in Sinhala, despite Tamil being his first language.

"Stop firing, stop firing, stop," his brains gave him the wrong signal.

My ambulance staff recognized Arjuna and confirmed that he was Tamil. Arjuna's brain froze with his last utterance.

"Stop firing, stop firing, stop," he continued to command.

Arjuna changed his tune and sang in Tamil. His brain was like a radio station, tuning into different stations: He switched back and forth from Sinhala to Tamil, like a wireless communication service. He constantly paused and replayed. The staff tuned into Arjuna's radio station with laughter. He entertained them by switching his lyrics from Tamil to Sinhala. Singing validated that his brain was still functioning. His brain spontaneously exploded with the impact of the bullet. I expected him to die in an hour. His brain responded in a bizarre manner. It was a fatal explosion. His head popped like fireworks. Air waves surged through his brains and his radio station continued to switch between Tamil and Sinhala.

I cleaned his wound. He was semiconscious. His brain marched to the beat of its own drums. It functioned in a unique matter. He sang Tamil lyrics perfectly. His mental focus was under siege. He spoke to the ambulance driver in Tamil. His brain definitely had a mind of its own.

I informed the Red Cross and other health organizations about Arjuna's condition. The United Nation's Health Ministry was ready to negotiate with the army. My ambulance driver was panic stricken. He was sceptical about transporting these patients to another hospital. I promised to ride along with him, to give him more confidence.

Arjuna continued to sing Tamil songs like a nightingale. His voice was robust and powerful. He sang about love and romance. He sang to his heart's content. His notes were complex. He sang about love. His songs indicated that his brains, was in good physical condition. His songs were emotional, and he had an excellent pitch control.

Arjuna was not aware that his wife was dead. I bandaged his head and sent him to Colombo. His wife was still in the ambulance, launched on the rock. Unfortunately, Arjuna passed away after five days, of brain injury. Just like Emperor Shah Jahan and his wife, Arjuna and his wife were buried side by side. It was an end to a perfect love story.

The other Sinhalese at my hospital feared the LTTE. I gave them all the comfort and support they needed. I pledged to keep them safe. Being in a LTTE area pose as a threat to them. They yearned to be reunited with their families. I called the Red Cross and the LTTE and conveyed the message that the Sinhalese patients needed to be reunited with their loved ones.

"These Sinhalese people are treated. They need to be reunited with their families," I conveyed the message to the Red Cross.

"The government army does not want to open up the area," they were concerned.

"Please call them on another line and beg please," I pleaded.

"Ok, the army will allow you only one hour to transport these people home," they had a sigh of relief.

"The army notified us that the Red Cross vehicle cannot go to the hospital," another Red Cross member was baffled.

"Did they give us an exchange spot?" I inquired.

"Yes, the army stated that the exchange spot would be about 2 to 3km away," he instructed me.

The Sinhalese people found trust in me. I showed them respect and found the capacity to trust me deeply. I had very little experience in driving, yet I promised to transport them with an ambulance. They followed me around the hospital affirming that they are safe in my presence. They embraced all aspects of my character traits. I was spontaneously open to their requests. I guaranteed them protection. They revealed the capacity to trust me. They were vulnerable and susceptible to trust.

I accompanied them to the point of exchange. They had no legitimate need to fear. I put loyalty into practice. They perceived that I was a trust worthy doctor, who did not discriminate. I did not allow myself to get trapped in a world full of deceit and hatred. I did not hesitate to treat anyone. My head agreed with my heart. I delivered happiness and good health to all. I leaped into the helpful mode. My patients recognized that I pursued an authentic and humble nature. I advocated for the safety of all mankind. I gained a sense of peace of mind by practising human rights.

A weight was lifted off my shoulders, when we reached the exchange point. The Red Cross was there to meet us with open arms. I did not stumble, because I was an inexperienced driver. I had precious cargo to deliver. They trusted in me. The roads were a hazard, but I did not falter.

"Thank you, thank you doctor. You are our guardian angel," they fell at my feet as if they were worshipping me.

"I am so happy that all of you are safe," they were my fellow humans who developed a secure attachment to me.

"We are Sinhalese and you are Tamil, yet you gave us so much of respect and sympathy. We cannot forget you doctor!" they bowed down to my feet in worship with an essence of respect.

"No need to thank me. That's my duty," I humbly acknowledged.

"God bless you doctor," they expressed a genuine foundation of love.

We bid farewell. I could not turn the ambulance around because it was a narrow road. The ambulance driver helped me, before he departed. The Red Cross members watched me. They were concerned about my safety in a conflict zone. They provided me with inspiration, as my ambulance vanished into the dusty roads. I was playing with fire. The coast was clear. I perceived no danger, as I drove back to the hospital.

I could hear both sides. The government army and the LTTE engaged in vicious combat. Hatred was in the air. Both sides had the axe to grind. They had grievances and resentment towards each other. Revenge was their modus operandi. It was a battle of nerves. Each side aimed to weaken the other. There was no room for negotiation. The United Nations, Red Cross, Amnesty International and other Human Rights groups were present to help them bury the hatchet. Peace was needed to stop the fighting.

Houses were shattered, and trees were rooted. The area resembled the valley of the ashes. The combustion of homes and trees left a residual of ash. Ash covered the area, creating an image of fifty shades of grey. I perceived that I was watching an old black and white movie. In fact, it resembled a cryptic scene from a haunted movie. The environment was desolate, dreary, deadly, and ashy. It was a deadly sight. Dead bodies were scattered all over. The sight had an impact of everlasting terror in my mind. War gave birth to psychopathic killers. The lack of colour made it legitimately scary. It was the act of raving lunatics. The government blundered in creating a peaceful, democratic country.

I felt as if I was Dr. Frankenstein, surrounded by the tomb of death. I was not going to succumb to fear or anxiety. The sight of dead bodies sprawled all over, became a norm. It was boundless evil impulses that lead to thousands dying. The scene was graphic, like a graphic novel. Dogs walked around aimlessly.

The fighting progressed to a critical stage. It was vicious. The government army advanced. The LTTE and the army brutally fought, with no limitations. The government army targeted Tamil civilians. People were displaced. About ten to fifteen causalities arrived at my hospital daily, during the displacement. People were scared as if they had reached the gates of hell. The situation was horrendous.

A river ran under a small bridge. It was a bridge over troubled waters. Close to the bridge, an extended family gathered to cook under a tree. In times of solace, they sought pleasure in being close together. They set aside the grievances of war, to enjoy each other's company. The ideology of hatred did not reside in their minds. Women cooked together under the tree, while the men and children narrated stories. They tried to maintain a normal setting, while surrounded by atrocities.

It was extremely disturbing when an army attack plane surfaced. The extended family went into flight mode and hid under the small bridge. The plane flew around them. It was not a conventional method of two armies fighting each other. This was a brutal massacre of innocent Tamil civilians. There were about ten people from the extended family, who perceived the little bridge as a place of safety. Like trolls, they hid under the bridge.

The military saw them and alerted their commander. The commander instructed them to fire. That ambush was a brutal massacre of genocide. They fired their artillery on the small bridge. The whole extended family was brutally killed. Their bodies were badly wounded. They could not be identified.

Their bodies were delivered to the hospital that night. Nobody moved! We saw bodies with organs oozing out of them. Tamil civilians were annihilated. Charred bodies were all over. They were human beings. That was the recipe for death. It was beyond the grave. How does one communicate with the dead? Their souls had moved beyond the veil. They were safe in a mysterious place above. They did not fulfill their bucket list before dying. The last on their list was cooking a conjoint meal, for an extended family. A whole family was exterminated. On that critical day, I testified... GENOCIDE! That was my note, from the No Fire Zone!

Amidst, the chaos of death, a six-year-old stood like the statue of liberty. She towered over the dead bodies. She was the symbol of freedom and liberty. She was the only sole survivor in the extended family. She was an enlightening spirit amongst torched bodies. Ironically, she held the torch to freedom. A little Tamil girl found freedom from a world of oppression. She stared at me with tears in her eyes. I reached out to her with comfort. I sent her to Batticaloa hospital to be treated. Her father picked her up; he was working that day, when his family was destroyed.

I took on the role of a mortician, because there was no one to take care of the bodies. I embalmed the bodies and arranged a burial service. I dressed the bodies up with hospital garments. The hospital staff took an active role in helping me bury the bodies.

This was a serious case of genocide. It was a human rights crime, yet nobody was accountable for it. I was like a magnet that attracted dead people. An entire group of Tamil civilians were brutally killed. They were denied their rights of freedom, because they belonged to the Tamil community of Sri Lanka. It was an obvious and devastating process of cleansing Sri Lanka of the Tamils. The aim of the government army was visible and obvious. Groups of innocent Tamils were harmed, tortured and killed. They were deliberately harmed physically, psychologically and socially. There were mass killings of Sri Lankan Tamils. Nobody, safe guarded them. Ethical and moral principals were dead. I testified that this was genocide.

After pulling these bodies to rest, my mind sang a song, as I witnessed genocide.

That night I cried,

Tamil civilians died,

Dead bodies I eyed,

I did not have pride,

There was no war guide,

Tamils forced to hide,

The Sri Lankan army lied,

Took the media for a ride,

It was a Tamil genocide,

By laws they did not abide,

In you I will confide,

What I saw was genocide,

Souls line up at my bedside,

It was like a tsunami tide,

The army and civilians collide,

United Nations can decide,

Sri Lankan government denied,

Their actions were genocide,

I saw what occurred inside,

We can vote on a landslide,

This is what I implied,

It was a Tamil genocide,

With all laws I complied,

The army did misguide,

Tamil civilians dead outside.

As a fatal war did preside,

Dead bodies on the roadside,

Tamil bodies on the seaside.

It was during low tide,

Testimony I did provide,

The truth has to be untied,

News has to be worldwide,

News has to be amplified,

News we cannot brush aside,

As a doctor I was certified,

Medicine was my civic pride,

It has to be clarified,

Dead bodies in the countryside,

Tamils were killed countrywide,

Not talking about the cyanide,

The army was not dignified,

What they did was falsified,

What doctors did use fortified,

I confess it was genocide,

War was a great divide,

Mass murders and homicide,

Tamil civilians were horrified,

Branded with an iron side,

Killing cannot be justified,

The situation should be magnified,

Answers have to be modified,

Tamils killed on the mountainside.

I admit I was mortified,

The Red Cross was mystified,

In the hospital beds multiplied,

All hospital beds were occupied,

Women and children, petrified,

Medical tools were not purified,

As a doctor I was qualified,

With the hospital... not satisfied,

My family life I set aside,

Life was not simplified,

Medicine is what I specified,

Medicines were not verified,

A nation was not unified,

To the United Nations I testified,

What the army did was genocide,

By fingerprint I was identified,

Torture on the 4th floor intensified,

With beatings they were preoccupied,

As Tamils we were classified,

I witnessed a Tamil genocide.

CHAPTER 9

Bridge over Troubled Waters

At the Eachchilampattu hospital, my sleeping arrangements were bizarre. I slept in a narrow corridor surrounded by four rooms for protection. The corridor was like my military trench, to protect me from the army. It sheltered me from any shelling or artillery attack. As the army advanced their tactics were brutal. They shelled anything and everything in their way. I felt as if I was in trench warfare. The corridor was surrounded by four rooms. The walls of the room were my defensive fortification. Like an underground bunker, I place heaps of soya bags against the wall, to fortify against any invasion from the army. The soya bags were meals for patients. It resembled sand bags. Most of the firing happened at night. I invited other staff members and patients to share my make belief corridor trench. It was complex enough to protect us against the constant threat of the army attacks. The soya bags were obstacles to protect us against shrapnel or bullets.

The army was brutal and inhospitable, when they drew closer to the hospital. It was horrendous when the LTTE advanced past the hospital. Such combat dominated the hospital vicinity. Like a rainbow formation, the LTTE and the army fired over the hospital at each other.

Swissh! Swissh! Swissh! An endless array of shelling passed the hospital. It was like Deepavali fireworks. The combat was dominated by the army, as the LTTE retreated. The army did not practise any obedience. They had no control over their firing. They did not impose discipline and even fired at innocent civilians. I realised that justice was not achieved, because casualties flooded the hospital like a tsunami wave. At all parts of the night, I treated civilians wounded by the army firing squad. The army was responsible for civilian deaths, execution style.

Patients, staff and I did not get enough sleep during the lulls of fighting. The artillery attacks induced fear in us. One night, heavy fighting was consistent. At about 3AM I heard a substantial loud bomb blast. This was followed by gruelling, hysterical screams. My instinct told me that the army had conducted an elaborate artillery attack on the civilians who lived under the bridge, for protection. I knew that the hospital would have an influx of severe civilian casualties. The bridge was a fortified area for civilians to hide.

I slept in my work clothing so that I was ready to receive casualties, throughout the night. The fundamental strategy of the army was to aim at Tamil civilians, as if cleansing the nation of the enemy. They waged war on innocent civilians under the bridge. It was conceived as a major offender. Without hesitation I ran into the wards of the hospital, with a sole purpose of welcoming patients.

The hospital was deserted like a haunted house. I ran around yelling.

"Hello... hello... is anyone here?" I tried to draw the attention of my staff.

"Hello... hello... is anyone here?" my voice came back to me in an echo.

"Hello please anyone... someone answer me!" I was in a state of panic.

"Yes" a vulnerable voice echoed through the ward.

"Where are you?" I raised my voice to complete with the bombardment.

"We are hiding in the toilet, doctor," they were safe.

"Why are you three young girls hiding in the toilet?" I was curious as three staff members emerged from the toilet, looking like lost puppies.

"The toilet is made of solid concrete. We thought we will be safe sleeping all night in the toilet," they chorused.

"Let's treat patients," I had a sense of emergency in my voice.

The staff got on all fours and we crawled around the hospital like stray dogs. The bombardment was severe. Like monsoon rain, the shells intensely fell outside the hospital. It rained bullets. The army and the LTTE were on either side of the hospital. I was shell shocked, with the intense shelling. The attacks and counter attacks were like music to our ears. We became masters of recognition. We could not deviate from the truth. Through the frequency of shelling, we were able to intercept the sounds. The sounds were distinct. We knew who manoeuvred the shelling. The sounds, which approached us from the army, were different to that of the LTTE. We were able to analyze their tactics and detect from which side the shelling originated. We acknowledged infiltration tactics of both sides.

The army took the initiative to attack the hospital successfully. When the intensity of the attack subsided, the damage to the hospital was evident. The army infiltration tactics were evident. The sun rose that morning to provide a spotlight on a hospital, which was war torn.

Tring... Tring... Tring... Tring... Tring...!

The sound of the phone was like an ambulance siren.

"Hi doctor, the bridge was shelled," I was notified.

"Are the people alright?" I was perturbed.

"No doctor, people crossed the river to Kathiraveli and Vaharai," he was distraught.

"The injured people are at Vaharai hospital," he was overwrought with anxiety.

"Who was responsible?" I was anxious.

"Doctor, the army shelled the bridge," he was perturbed,

"Doctor, you need to come to Vaharai hospital," another staff member was edgy.

Without hesitation I prepared an ambulance with medical equipment and rapidly made my way to Vaharai hospital. Our journey took us across the river on a ferry boat. As we neared Vaharai, I was bewilded to see thousands of people under the trees. It was like an ocean of people. They were homeless, cooking under the trees. People escaped from the Eachchilampattu area due to the shelling. I was scheduled to stay at the Vaharai hospital for a fort-night. I assumed that the LTTE would retrieve the Eachchilampattu area. I sent my ambulance and staff to bring back the medical equipment and medication, which I needed. The heat was stifling, as relentless civilians were sandwiched between Neem trees.

Prior to the use of Vaharai hospital, there was an authentic two-story hospital. In a typically tropical climate, the Neem trees with its every green leaves and elegant trunks surrounded the new hospital. The Neem trees provided an aesthetic value to the area. There was a Ganesha Temple close by, which used the branches of the Neem Trees to spiritually purify the area. Ironically, the Neem trees were also used for its miraculous medicinal purpose. It elicited great pleasure in its aesthetic values. The hospital overlooked the beach, which increased its sentimental value. The opening of the hospital was on January 2005, as scheduled: Unfortunately, on December 26, 2004 a massive Tsunami destroyed the hospital. The LTTE controlled area was subjected to jinx, as bad fortune fell upon its people, during the Tsunami and the war. The streak of bad luck visited the people twice, with a few years apart.

The area was visited by the MSF and the IRC. Both humanitarian organizations, Medicines Sans Frontieres (Doctors Without Borders) and the Italian Red Cross, played a vital role in transporting patients from Vaharai hospital to Batticaloa, about two hours away. The political instability prevented the IRC from travelling to Vaharai hospital. I obtained permission from the IRC and the United Nations, to offer my dedicated care to patients at the hospital. Eventually, the IRC returned with four doctors. That provided me with the opportunity to collaborate with the community, providing them with health education and prevention measures. I also provided assessment and inspired leadership to the Kathiraveli Health Centre. I used my competency, to enhance the Health Care centre, by providing an outpatient unit, medication and medical help. I dealt with complex issues at the pregnant mother clinics, providing them with counselling and supervision. I helped them overcome challenges and methods of enhancing their social growth.

The United Nation displayed moral obligations by working around the clock, to help those Sri Lankans displaced during the war. They were virtuous in implementing ideas, to protect the civilians displaced during the war. They recognized the notion of right for all people, according to the Universal laws and principles. Their benevolence brought smiles to faces of displaced Sri Lankans. They pursued actions to promote the well-being of all people. Their genuine help maximized the effort to promote human rights and human dignity. They motivated me to engage in the act of helping. Their cooperation was phenomenal.

The Red Cross also played a vital role in increasing the welfare of the people. They displayed empathy in treating patients. They were motivated by the survival of Sri Lankan civilians. They stood in the face of danger to save lives. They helped those whose lives were at stake. They played a dominant role in helping those in distress. Each time I called them for help, they provided me with a sense of oneness.

UNICEF engaged in the same motive to promote survivals. Working with them provided me with the potential to support the injured. They were there to help the less fortunate Sri Lankans, in the war zone. Civilians were threatened by the shortage of food. My social exchange with them helped them provide for others.

Oxfam played an integral role in providing water. They focused on human biological needs. They were good Samaritans whose prime concern was to help those displaced during the war. They helped me with my random medical assignments with the community.

My mediation with all the humanitarian groups helped relieve distress. The degree of their help impacted all Sri Lankans. Like a pressure cooker, they all worked with limited time. They provided me with the social reinforcement, to help any injured civilians. The war zone was potentially dangerous for all of them. Their commitment and dedication service were obvious. In cases of emergency I called them. They helped me follow particular guidelines in the most critical situations. They helped me shape into a positive person. They were my role models, who encouraged me to help others.

They extrinsically motivated me to exceed my duties as a medical doctor. I helped run the administration, run the hospital, deal with the patients and serve children. Cooperation with the staff and other humanitarian organizations was integral for all to be happy. I was happy to be on call for 24 hours. It reinforced the principles of helping others in need.

The day I developed a severe fever, I continued to work. I could not sleep, knowing that the patients needed me. The golden rule was to save lives. Patients arrived at all parts of the night. They kept my mind occupied, so I did not focus on my own illness. My patients provided me with all the inner strength and physical competence, to work at all hours. The viral fever and flu were my uninvited guests, who I had to ignore.

News informed me that the IDP camp at Kathiraveli was bombed. November 7, 2006, eighty shells were fired by the Sri Lankan army according to witnesses. Artillery was fired at a school. The army claimed that the LTTE fired from a school zone. According to the Human Rights Watch, the LTTE was not present in the area. They concluded that army intentionally fired artillery at the IDP camp and school.

The SLMM visited the coastal village of Kathiraveli in Vaharai, part of the Batticaloa district and confirmed that the LTTE was not present in the area. This catastrophic shelling killed many and wounded hundreds of Tamil civilians. A number of Tamil civilians housed at a school were intentionally attacked. It brought me to tears to note that the Sonobo Children's Home was also shelled, injuring infants. War waged against innocent Tamil infants.

Kathiravel was populated with Tamils and Vedda people. The army blamed the LTTE, for using Tamil civilians as human shields. The Sri Lankan Monitoring Mission proclaimed that the LTTE was not present in the area. The LTTE was stationed at the Sinnakangai camp, about 2km away.

The hospital turned into a disaster zone, with no space for patients. I treated all the patients who arrived with care. There were delays to transport some to the hospitals because the ambulance drivers were afraid to enter the area.

The government denied the attack. Human Rights organizations could not enter the area because of government blocks. Ambulances and the United Nations Food program could not pass through. I contacted the Red Cross to deliver more ambulances. The incident happened at 11:30 am. The ambulances were only allowed to pass the government checkpoints at 4 pm.

It was pandemonium. Red was the dominant colour at the hospital. A stream of blood flowed like a river. I was covered in blood. Tamil blood with its genetic composition was all over. Bloodshed was all over the hospital. It evoked my visual imagery as I observed streams of blood, making its way down the hospital corridors like tributaries. I asked the government to send me blood to conduct operations. On a figurative note, the irony was that I did receive blood on a whole new scale. The government delivered blood through injured patients.

I observed the palm of my hands covered in blood like a serial killer. It was difficult to endure the sight of blood. It was the flesh and blood of my own Tamil community. The bad blood between the government and the Tamil civilians was obvious. Blood rushed to my head, as I looked around at the injured. All the bloodshed was symbolic of hatred. With blood, sweat and tears, I tried to save lives. The Sri Lankan government accused the LTTE of drawing the first blood. In defence, the LTTE claimed that they did not have Tamil blood in their hands. It was cold blooded murder on the path of the army. It made my blood curdle to see such disaster. It made my blood boil to count the dead. My blood ran cold, as more and more patients came into the hospital. Parents cried hysterically to see their own flesh and blood deceased. The situation was bloody.

CHAPTER 10

The White Flag

We carried the waving flag, as a sign of our freedom. The army advised me to instruct the Tamil people to create white flags, out of pieces of clothing. There were about twenty thousand displaced people. I had to send twenty-five at a time with their white flags. People with no shoes and very little clothing began their march at about 5AM.

It was a walk to freedom. People headed to the lagoon. They had to cross over by ferry, to seek safety in Maankerny. The Panichchankeny Bridge in the vicinity was destroyed by the LTTE. Their objective was to prevent the army from crossing over. Good Samaritans in Maankerny waited to receive the people. Farm tractors, agricultural vehicles, busses and three wheelers transported people through the jungle. I chose to send the old Tamil civilians through the jungle via the heavy vehicles. Family members clustered together. There were two hundred vehicles to transport people though the dangerous jungle.

The United Nations were there to support the people. I was the last one standing. I patrolled through the hospital wards, to confirm that there was no one left. As people trudged through the jungle, I wandered through the hospital. When I was confident that everyone left, I called the United Nations to touch base and I notified them.

"Hello, this is Dr. V, I am calling to inform you that I kept to my word. I am the last one at the hospital," fear was in my voice.

"Are you ready to depart from the war zone," a member of the United Nations was concerned.

"I was threatened on the phone. The government did not want me to talk to the media," I felt intimidated.

Just before I could depart on my long journey I got a call from a paramilitary group. There were two paramilitary groups in Sri Lanka. A member of the EPDP paramilitary group, called me but chose to remain anonymous. At first, he adopted a friendly tone.

"Doctor why don't you talk to the LTTE to stop fighting," he tried to brainwash me.

"I am a doctor not a politician. It is a politician's duty to talk to the LTTE. I am not a mediator. I have zero power to stop the LTTE from fighting," my voice was sharp as a razor edge.

"You bleep bleep,bleep,bleep,bleep! I know that you are a LTTE, working for the LTTE," obscene language exited though his mouth, like bullets through a gun.

"I do not belong to the LTTE," I kept calm as he raised his voice with aggression.

"You bleep bleep, bleep!" profanities burst out of his mouth, like verbal diarrhea.

"This conversation is not necessary. I am only a medical doctor," it was as if I had to take an oath.

He continued to curse me with the four-letter word, with disrespect. Such obscenity was part of his foul vocabulary. I did not let his blasphemy taint my professional demeanour.

I was guilty of saving the people. They did not approve of that. Like a wheel I was the axis. My people depended on me. It disturbed the army that people followed me. My good intention was to save people in contrast to the army, whose intention was to kill. The paramilitary group Karuna jeopardized my life.

Like a school of sardines, I packed people into a fishing boat. The hook was to send them to safety. The Karuna group informed my people that they would kill me. I had to dodge their bullet. My instinct informed me that if I was not present, they would kill my people, innocent Tamil civilians. I was their guardian angel, assigned to protect them. I was always available to all citizens, in times of difficulties.

The divine spirit bestowed upon me the power to protect others. The United Nations was my guardian angels, watching over me, though each phase of the war. I lit up their path, as they transitioned to freedom. I carried the torch to ensure protection for all.

Like an Olympic torch, I kept the flame burning for all civilians. The sacred fire burned in my heart, in honour of my people. I was the witness that the military feared. I spilled the beans, when I spoke to the international media. The paramilitary contacted my friend.

"Hello, you the friend of Dr. Varatharajah?" they probed.

"Yes," my friend affirmed.

"Dr. Varatharajah is so young. He is wasting his life. Tell him to leave. Tell him to take a boat and we will save him," they tried to govern my movements.

"Ok," my friend noted their supremacy.

"If he does not stop, we will kill him, you hear?" my friend took the clout for me.

"In other words, he is the witness you fear," my friend was bold.

"We will kill him," it was an imprint in the mind of my friend.

"That makes me a witness, then," he advocated for me.

I realised that their intention was evil. I had to conceal my profession and disguise as a civilian, as I embarked on my journey. I dressed up as a civilian to avoid danger. My façade was imperative. I had to hide behind a smoke screen.

I recalled that the night before I departed, I received a caution from a member of the LTTE.

"Hello doctor," with urge in his voice.

"Yes Dr. Varatharajah," I suspected a red flag.

"If you go to the army-controlled area, the paramilitary is planning to kill you," they gave me a heads up.

"I know that they will kill me, but I am here to save my people," I was sincere.

"We can help you. We will carry you on a stretcher, for your own safety," it was forewarning.

"No, it is okay if they kill me. I will sacrifice my life for my people," I was adamant.

"But we can save you," he was steadfast.

They were insistent. I did not compromise. I asked to be recognised as a civilian. My people walked alongside me on the warm sand of the beach. I had my own modus operandi.

The army used the people as human shields, to advance their military forced. The army marched behind the people towards the LTTE controlled area of Vaharai. The army used the people as a motive to advance.

My staff, people, patients and all the civilians pledged to be with me until we reached our destination. I felt secure, as they insured my safety. We bonded like glue to paper. We had an amazing relationship based on trust. Trust was the core factor in our bonding. Trust enabled us to respect each other. Trust placed us on a spiritual dimension. It came with positivity, love and emotional bonding. With trust we emerged together as one strong team, ready to help each other.

Trust emerged when a civilian insisted that I use his motor bike, on the journey. He felt that I would be safe on the motor bike and blend in with the civilians. Another civilian bestowed trust upon me, when she handed me her baby. The meaning of love and trust was articulated at that moment. She believed that clutching her baby would allow me to blend in with the civilians. They thrived on seeing me safe. My social functioning was a variable based on their safety as well. I clutched onto the baby, while on the motorbike. The benevolence was based on oral obligations and integrity. They tried to hide my identity, to keep me safe. They invested in my life.

Tamil civilians with their white flags marched ahead of me on foot. Suddenly, the Tamil civilians were crippled with fear. They were paralyzed with fear. Fear inherently brought on chronic stress. Their marching came to a sudden halt, when they were stopped by the army. Anxiety floated through the crowd like a wave. Like a contagious disease, fear spread through the crowd. Confronted by the army was like confronting a wild animal. They were in fight or flight mode. Fear coupled with anger surrounded them. They perceived that they were going to be killed by the army. The situation was dangerous. Their reaction was panic. Anger and anticipated anxiety altered their mental functioning.

The problem was amplified because the Tamil civilians could not speak Sinhala. The army could not speak Tamil. There was no translator around. I could not conceal my identity, because I was a man on the run. I felt a turbulence of emotion. My blood pressure launched like a rocket. I knew that they would kill me. My fear was overwhelming. Hopelessness blew through the crow causing emotional paralysis.

"Doctor, doctor come here," an innocent old lady yelled waving her finger in my direction.

"Oh God, now they know that I am a doctor," I whispered as I confronted a threat.

"Doctor you can speak Sinhala, come," she bravely pointed at me as I prepared to enter combat with the army.

"Yes, doctor come translate," was an army official's response.

"Yes," I was induced with fear, as the cat was out of the bag.

"Come here doctor," his tone was friendly.

"Yes… yes… yes… yes," I shuttered, as I anticipated danger.

"Why are you stopping us?" I translated in Sinhala.

"Doctor, we need to clear the landmines before the people pass by," he explained in a concerned tone.

"People are afraid that they will be sent back to Vaharai," I translated and relayed the message to the people.

"Do not worry, you now have clearance to walk," they instructed, maintaining a friendly tone.

That was a close call. I felt as if I dodged the bullet. Nevertheless, I was always a doctor on call. It was my spiritual calling to protect people.

I got onto my motorbike, which was a symbol of freedom and progress. The wind blew through my hair. I found a new sense of confidence and protection. The road dipped and curved. I conquered all my fears, as I cut through the air with agility and speed. I lost those nerves and cluttered thoughts, as it blew away with the wind. I felt like an eagle soaring through the air. I cut through the air, as meticulous as a surgeon cutting through flesh. I felt safe on my miracle on wheels.

I passed the road of happiness and entered the road of bliss, knowing that I was leading my Tamil people to safety.

My journey ended at a broken bridge. Several busses were stationed at the Panichchankerny Bridge. My lens zoomed in to a paramilitary group who mingled with the army. It evoked my sense of sight as I noticed that the area was bombed. Trees continued to burn. It was another valley of the Ashes, with various shades of grey. I felt like a colored image in a black and white movie. Burnt ash was the predominant sight. The sight was devastating.

It was frightening for the people. It felt as if we entered into futuristic apocalypse. It felt as if the heavens would open up to reveal, the secret of our next journey. It was a spiritual vision of the final destruction of earth. I saw this image in movies. In reality, it was a catastrophic sight of the detrimental effect of war, on humanity. It employed new meaning to life in Sri Lanka.

I felt like a phoenix arising from the ashes. I wished that beyond the combustion, we would have a renewal of life. I wished that the sun would rise and wrap its rays like arms, around my people.

Life became more dramatic when we encountered a new army place at Maankerny. People were stopped at that point. They recognized me as the doctor. Their intention was friendly. I was met by journalist and the military media, who interviewed me.

"Why did you work there?" it was their routine question.

"I am a government doctor," the answer was obvious.

"How do you feel?" was the next question.

"I am worried about my people. They need food, shelter and medical treatment," I was sincere.

"Why sacrifice your life to make this journey?" they knew little about human rights.

"I am a doctor. It is my duty to work in the war zone to save lives," the truth was exposed, as I answered several superficial questions.

We walked for six hours. We finally reached the Valaichchenai hospital. It was an army control area. The doctor at the hospital welcomed me. I handed the boy back to his mother, who fell at my feet as a sign of respect and gratitude. I settled down in the doctor's quarters and there was a mobile clinic for the people.

Images of the war were like a slide in my mind. I felt safe until 6pm when my doctor colleague received a call. He could not put on a poker face. His anxiety showed. There was an open threat from the paramilitary group. Fear revisited me. They were looking for me and planned to visit the hospital in an hour. They were going to send the Karuna group to kill me. We had to think fast as my safety was in question.

"Doctor, come with me," an Italian Red Cross personal offered help.

"This Italian Red Cross person lives in the Tsunami destroyed area. the army and paramilitary would not visit that area," the doctor notified me with top secrecy.

"If anyone asks about you we would say that you arrived and left. Nobody knows about your whereabouts," the Italian Red Cross person offered his solutions to my problem.

"I feel fear. At the same time, I am worried about my people," I shook with fear.

"The civilians are safe here. Most of them were sent to school buildings and IDP camps. Do not worry. They have food and shelter too. After registration and paper work they will be allowed to live with relatives," they consoled me.

An area destroyed by the December 26, 2004 tsunami was Valaichenai. The tsunami was the inciting force behind the devastation. The death toll was in the thousands. The massive waves swallowed up people, homes buildings and infrastructure. The water surged through Valaichchenai, uprooting everything in its path. About thirty-metre-tall waves, like a massive maniac monster, crushed everything in its path. The tsunami was triggered by a massive earthquake, with a magnitude of

9.0 on the Richter scale. The Indian Ocean rose to power, killing thousands of people in the Batticaloa District. Roads were washed away making it difficult to enter the area.

I headed to the Valaichchenai area, in the Batticaloa district, under cover. I wore a full covered helmet to disguise myself. I was a fugitive, in my own country. The IRC official transported me to the United Nations office. Although my situation was dangerous, the United Nations always provided me with protection.

"What is your age doctor?" a Caucasian woman who worked there was curious.

"I am 30 years old madam," I expressed.

"That young and you gave up your personal life to help others?" she was in shock.

"Yes madam," I was humble.

"We are surprised about your story and situation," she expressed solidarity.

"My people came first, before my personal life," I truthfully claimed my responsibility.

When we were ready to leave with the IRC official, another motorbike cut us off. My heart skipped a beat. I pressed the panic button and fear invaded my body like a disease. It was a major setback, as the man on the motor bike scrutinized me. I lost control over reality. I panicked like a frightened horse. I knew that I could not dodge the bullet at such a close range. Fear and anxiety rolled in like those huge tsunami waves. My breathing increased, and my body was wet with perspiration. I trembled like an earthquake as my heart rate increased. I was in a situation of imminent danger. I wondered if a heart attack would kill me before the bullet. I imagined that the sight of a trigger would trigger a heart attack. Several medical theories were imprinted in my mind like a textbook.

"Dr. Varatharajah!" his sharp voice was like a bullet to my brain.

"Hands up," it was as if I spoke for him.

"Hahaha hahahaa!" he laughed like a creepy clown from scary movie.

"Dr. Varatharajah!" his voice was like an emergency siren.

"My hands are up," I cried as if it was my final farewell.

"I recognized you from a distant," his white teeth glowed.

"Yes," my voice took a leave of absence.

"It's me, your friend from school," those words were like an anti-anxiety medication.

"Yes, I remember you. How are you? It's been a long time. You scared me to death," we laughed, as if the joke was on me.

The rhythm of laughter filled the air. I laughed as if someone tickled me. Laughter became contagious and the IRC officials laughed as if he was in pain. Laughter was the medicine, which cured my anxiety and fear.

Thereafter, I had to report on duty at the Trincomalee District located on the northwest coast of Sri Lanka. It was my hometown. I reported there to fill a position as a director of the hospital. There were more than ten checkpoints to get there. The army checked the passengers of the buses that passed through. The fear of being arrested crossed my mind. My whereabouts was unknown. However, there was a search for me. They wanted to arrest me and kill me. I approached the Batticaloa health director, who I worked for, at one stage. I asked him to help me with transportation. I believed that I would be safe if I was transported by ambulance or a health department vehicle. I explored all avenues, to stay safe.

The health director was extremely friendly, when I was in Vaharai. I believed that he would help me on humanitarian grounds. He was also a friend and fellow doctor. I begged for help but was turned down. He did not help me on grounds of being in a different district. I felt hurt. I was a doctor from the war zone who worked for twenty-four hours, yet unappreciated. He had the power but refused to exert such power. My personal safety was at risk.

My time of arrest was drawing near. I had no phone. I could not contact my transportation driver. Time was not in my favour. I was close to death. I looked up and wondered if the heaven's gates would open up for me. All I could think about was that I put my life on the line to help others and there was no one to help me. That magnanimous quality in me was still alive. Nobody could defeat the generosity of my spirit. My bleeding heart still revealed sympathy. I had to find a diplomatic way to solve my problems.

I was skating on thin ice. Danger was on all around me. I walked on dangerous grounds. If I was arrested, it would lead to negative consequences. As time passed, I sailed close to the wind. My situation, at that time was critical. I desperately needed to go to the Trincomalee District. A desolate feeling came over me. My thoughts were forlorn. The inner notion of being closed to my family crossed my mind. I was in a path of isolation. Sadness filled my heart. I felt as if I was isolated with a deadly virus.

With help I finally contacted UNICEF. They understood the story I narrated to them. They realized that I needed to go to Trincomalee urgently. I longed for my family. I needed to work at the hospital. They showed empathy and agreed with my plans. They went out of their way to direct me to safety.

As a fugitive, with strict coordination I set on a mission to get to Trincomalee. Homeward bound was a difficult mission. Undercover, I constantly changed vehicles, to assure that I was not being followed. I felt as if I was in a relay race, changing batons. At several points there was a car waiting for me. Like a mouse observing my surroundings, I darted from one car into another. The Gods watched from above. The Universe provided me with protection.

At one stage, I was educed with fear, when I got into one car. I wondered if I was in the wrong car. The driver did not say a word. He stared at me in his review mirror with piercing eyes and sped away. The world spun around me, as fear set in. I felt as if I had to negotiate with fear. I turned up my collar as if it was a shield of protection, to disguise my face. I was anxious and confused. The battle between the army and the LTTE was notorious. However, my inner battle with fear was more challenging. My self-confidence took a leave of absence. I developed a phobia for cars that parked next to me, at the street light. I attempted to focus on my breathing. The sound of my deep breathing was like a gust of wind. My heavy breathing drew the attention of the driver. He looked at me through his review mirror and we locked eyes. It was as if my breathing was contagious, because his breathing became as heavy as mine. Our breathing blended in like symphony, with rhythm and texture. It denoted how tense we were. In the silence of the moment, our breathing was like background music. The incessant flow of our breathing broke the dead silence. Fear assaulted my inner peace. Fear took siege of my entire body. Silence terrified me. Ironically, thoughts of visiting a Hindu temple introduced me to silence. In that situation silence brought me Zen and profound inner peace.

I longed for the sanctuary of home. I was homeward bound. Home where my heart was! I longed to be with my wife and parents. The driver winked at me through his review mirror. For the first time he had a smile across his face. I looked at him spellbound, with a gloomy face.

"Welcome to Thampalakamam," he whispered.

"Thampalakamam," I smiled for the first time after the long journey.

I felt like a soldier returning home from a war. It was home, sweet home. I embarked on a dangerous journey, to arrive at my place of retreat. Anxiety and fear escaped. My spirit was replenished with positive energy. Home was my positive and spiritual haven. It uplifted my spirit when I entered my serene home. There to meet me were my aunt and wife. Reconciliation mingled with tears and joy. Gratefulness, appreciation, compassion and gratitude, followed me through the doors of my home.

The next day I got a call from a Sinhalese journalist Mr. G. He worked with the associate press. He worried about my personal life. Mr. G brought me wisdom, peace of mind and happiness. I was blessed to have him as a friend. He brought me spiritual enlightenment, as he tried to alleviate my pain. He brought me to self-realization that Tamils and Sinhalese could bond together in love, peace and harmony. He helped me overcome my anxiety and fear. We bonded like two peas in a pod. I was an integral part of his life. We tapped into each other's spiritual energy. Peace was an important component to bring the Sri Lankan people together as one. My dear friend Mr. G illuminated and explored every form of soul searching. We kept in touch.

I reached out for transportation to visit the health department. My hometown Thampalakamam was in Trincomalee District in Sri Lanka. It was on the south west area. Ancient mythology glamourized it as a prosperous and large village known as Tampainakar, which housed the Koneswaram Temple. The civil war in the 1980's and 1990's impacted the area, with massacres and displacement. In 2002 it sprung up to life, housing many Hindus.

I went to meet the regional health director at the health department. I wrote a letter to him briefing him about medical inventory. I proposed that I wanted to be transferred to the Trincomalee Hospital. I was assigned to work in the maternity ward. It was a stable place in a government-controlled area.

Nevertheless, calls continued to pour in from Batticaloa. Unknown people searched for me. They gathered information about my personal life. The paramilitary planned to kill me in about three days. The Karuna group made open threats.

The day I was going to begin working as a medical doctor in the new hospital, a staff member was scheduled to work with me. She was a young girl of 25 years old, who was my assistant nurse. She was excited about arriving at the hospital early to fulfill her medical duties. I was excited about training her to treat the patients, to the best of her ability.

On her way to the hospital she was intercepted by the paramilitary group, Karuna. It was believed that her friends provided the Karuna group with personal information. Hell broke loose. It was a terrifying ordeal. They intruded into her privacy. Around her lunch time she was kidnapped. They confronted her on the street. She was threatened and floored by the group. The Karuna group prowled the streets in search of her. It prompted outrange within the medical community. Her abduction was directly linked to me.

"Do you know Dr. Varatharajah?" they probed for information.

"I am new. I have not met him as yet," danger surrounded her.

"You are holding information from us," they mimed as if they would carve out her flesh.

"No, no, let me go," she fought them off.

"We are going to kill him. We need to know about his whereabouts," her abductors were ruthless, raw and uncouth.

She was transported to the police station. She fought the abductors to save her life. Danger followed her like a shadow. The director rushed to the police station at about 9pm.

At the time of the incident, I was at home. Mr. G, my Sinhalese friend was there to help and escort me. His loyalty and kindness brought me peace of mind; He gave my number to the Humanitarian Organizations. They were a breath of fresh air. Their kindness and generosity were impeccable. They demonstrated the highest form of propriety. They made themselves available to me at all times. I was so grateful for their flawless nature. They had a great impact on encouraging me to escape from Sri Lanka. My life was in danger. They were present for all my beckoned needs.

They coaxed my wife and I into travelling to Colombo to apply for a passport. They extended their kind gesture, by providing us with transport. They enticed me to leave unconditionally. When I returned to the Trincomalee hospital, staff members warned me about several phone calls, which they received. The caller always asked personal information about me and my whereabouts.

On that Friday, I slept at the hospital. I had no peace of mind. Thoughts ran through my mind, like a marathon. My literal plans collided with my soul's plans. I provided myself with multiple choice answers and questions. My existence was traumatic to me and those around me. I prompted myself to choose the correct answer wisely:

What do I do with my life?

    a) Escape from Sri Lanka
    b) Escape to an LTTE area, Mullaittivu
    c) Commit suicide

Those were the three most profound answers, to my challenging experience. I had nightmares. Plan A was enticing. Plan B was logical. Plan C provided me with a deeper meaning of life. Plan A was a proposal from the Human Rights Organization. Plan B was subject to my own inner soul.

The possibility and probability of plan C set me into a state of chronic depression. It was a changing point in my life. I was in ultimate danger, to all those around me. It was a love hate relationship, I encountered with life. The highest intention of my soul was to dedicate myself in treating patients and my profession grew like a seed in my heart. The army and the paramilitary groups visibly hated me, for saving the Tamil civilians. It was a bitter sweet decision, which was imposed upon me. Suicide was evil over triumph. My wisdom motivated me to show self-loyalty. My soul advised me to reject self-betrayal. Images of light and dark surrounded me. It was a complex inner dialogue within me.

I wandered around the darkness of my room, in a state of confusion. I engaged in a conversation with myself like a Shakespeare's soliloquy. The famous soliloquy from Hamlet visited my fragile mid,

"To be or not to be. To live or to die?"

I was in a state of limbo. I wandered around the room in a state of wonder.

My mind sang a song of shame:

Suicide is a shame,

Now who is to blame?

A state of depression,

The need for confession,

Death is not a choice,

Listen to the inner voice,

The emotional pain,

Tears shed like rain,

And that emotional mind,

Inner peace you can find,

Do not give in to stress,

Modify feelings of distress,

Do not put on a poker face,

Life- you have to embrace,

Look to your spiritual needs,

Fulfill those spiritual deeds,

Suicide is not the end,

Avoid that dangerous bend,

And thoughts of suicide,

In friends you can confide,

Misery in a black hole,

Climb up the happy hole,

Do not give in to grief,

Life cannot be so brief,

Imbalance in the brain,

It's like a derailed train,

That pain you can endure,

Spiritual love is a cure,

The military breeds fear,

Your protection is so near.

Plan C was definitely not my choice under any circumstances. I had too much to live for. My inner wisdom led me to plan B. Plan B led me to Mullaittivu. The universe sent me blessings as I boarded a government bus. It was a top secret. My parents and in-laws were in that area. I would not become an outlaw in that area. My wife had an operation and was in no condition to travel. Equipped with a small bag of necessities, I progressed on my journey. I boarded a bus a 6 AM to Vavuniya. I placed my stethoscope at the top of my bag. It was my passport to safety. My stethoscope was my symbol of identification. Doctors did not travel on the public bus. I crossed a checkpoint, which made me uneasy.

They filtered everyone, as if using a microscope to identify bacteria. I asked for an ambulance at that point. I travelled by ambulance to Mullaittivu.

In Mullaittivu, the plot thickened. I was not aware that an ambulance driver transported his personal items in an ambulance. The emergency service had strict protocols. Ambulances were designated for the transport of patients only. The policies implemented that no personal belongings, were allowed to be transported in an ambulance.

The ambulance driver was stopped and arrested for the misuse of an EMS vehicle. All the items in the vehicle were confiscated by the police. He had to appeal in court on several occasions. He did not know that I was on my way to the area. He narrated a story to the judge that the personal items belonged to me. To add fuel to the fire, he forged my signature in a legal court document, stating that all items belonged to me.

The ambulance driver confessed about his wrong doings to me. In the time of war, I felt that I had the moral obligation to defend him. The ambulance driver narrated his story to me as if he was a sinner making a confession to a priest. I acknowledged his wrong doing and respected his honest confession. I appeared in court before the judge and other police officials. I spoke to them in Sinhalese.

They were all so friendly and most of all were impressed to meet me. The judge released all the items.

I went where no man wanted to go. I requested to be a doctor at the Mullaittivu hospital. No doctor wanted to work at that hospital. For one month, I worked at the hospital with no salary. I felt a little safe in the area. Although there were still threats against my life, in the government control areas, I did not face severe problems at that time.

CHAPTER 11

Mother's love

A flashback made me ponder on a story so close to my heart. I recall when I stood at the window of the Eachehilampattu Hospital, the emerald green waters of the Indian Ocean, mingled with the sugar like sand of the beach. It was a flawless image of the waves, which played a game of hide and seek. Fluffy, foamy, floating, white waves rolled over the sand the retreated as if teasing the shore. Towering waves rolled in like galloping white horses. Children hopped, skipped and jumped as the waves surfaced on shore. They picked up an array of beautiful beige shells. The pristine white sand shimmered like diamonds in the sun. That was mans' paradise. The glimpse of the beautiful clear water was like a painting. The spectacular beaches with the elegant tall palm trees, complimented the coastline. Beach goers covered their feet in a blanket of sand, which stretch for miles. With the civil war raging close by, it had to be paradise lost.

Fisherman perched themselves on little boats. Their fishing rods resembled the bent over coconut, palm trees. Their skill and balance were like professional acrobats. It was an iconic picture. Slender grown men with mocha skins, threw their baits into the spectacular sea. It was a picture of beauty and the beast. The fishermen were the beast, attacking the waters in search of fish. The cool waters protected them from the excruciating hot rays of the sun. They resembled gingerbread men, baking in the hot sun. My eyes zoomed in like camera lens. I recorded every picturesque, glorious and breathtaking image in my mind. My eyes were like a GoPro, dramatically capturing the dazzling and astounding moment. It was a picture of Sri Lanka at its best. It was mesmerizing. It was a picture that would enthral any tourist.

I imagined the Sri Lankan mythology, of the handsome Sinhalese Prince Vijaya, falling in love with the Tamil Princess Kuveni, on that enchanting beach.

I had to focus on another part of reality, which was treating patients. Kumaran Master from the Eastern province worked for the LTTE. He was friendly. He was from Jaffna but resided in the Eastern province. He worked for the LTTE for a long time and was ready for marriage. His marriage was arranged with Ananthy, as they made a suitable match. In 2005 they married in an LTTE area in Muthur. In June 2006, I was stationed at the Eachehilampattu Hospital, when Ananthy was rushed in and delivered a beautiful, bouncy, baby girl. After two days she was released from the maternity ward. After two days Kumaran registered the baby at the hospital. Their kindness and appreciation were genuine. They were an authentic couple, who visited the hospital on regular routine check-ups and for the baby's vaccination.

An innocent baby girl brought the parents joy and happiness. The baby was born into a world that was devious, deceptive, dangerous and selfish. The cold cruel created circumstances flawed the beauty of childbirth. It was an escalated punishment for the innocent baby. The loss of innocence was evident. A child with pure intentions was challenged by the brutal acts of war. The war did not come to a halt because a child was born. The bombing, shelling and fighting was the contemporary image, which surrounded the child. It was a powerful message to the world, that the concept of innocence was challenged. An innocent child born into the circumstances of war would grow up to bear grudges on the antagonist.

My story moved from Eachehilampattu to Vaharai hospital. The displacement of people from Muthu to Vaharai was vast. There were about seventy thousand people in that vicinity. The access to medication was limited. The war contributed to displacement and suffering. There were lack of bunkers, food, shelters and transportation. There were asylum seekers, who fled the country in search of protection, as refugees.

The call for duty, took Kumaran away from his wife and baby. Ananthy and the baby lived with her parents, under devastating circumstances. They struggled with internal displacement. Under the brutal circumstances of war, they were forced to live under trees and bridges. The instability of war placed LTTE family members, in clustered small areas around a well. The burden of suffering surrounded them. They created makeshift tents as their homes, with no lavatory facilities. They were forced to use the nearby bushes as outside toilets. Since the area housed about seventy thousand people, poor hygienic conditions pursued. There were restrictions on times to cook or feed. It was persecution for them. People who were forcibly displaced lived in fear. There was no way to resolve the crisis as the army used heavy artillery, at a close proximity. Family members were killed in the open conflict. Danger surrounded them.

The army closed the roads to the hospital, which made them vulnerable. They were burdened with suffering. The illustration of cruelty was evident when the government army played psychological games with the Tamil civilians. They coaxed them on, to get food. When they arrived at a certain destination, they were cunningly turned away. They lived in total poverty, with no means of obtaining food or milk powder for the babies. Money and groceries were limited. Displacement caused devastation. Ethnic cleansing and coerced displacement increased poverty. Human rights were what they needed, to survive.

I had my own doctor's resident to eat and sleep. This made me feel guilty because I cared for everyone. Their basic human needs were repressed. They lived in inhumane conditions, exposed to physical and psychological devastation. Their personal safety and security were threatened. The situation was dangerous and horrifying.

Tamil civilians were targeted by the army. No line was drawn between the LTTE and the Tamil civilians. Artillery fire, shelling and bombing were not confined to the battlefield. The army strategically targeted the Tamil civilians. Forced expulsions motivated people to escape from the LTTE controlled areas to the government-controlled areas.

The threat of danger overpowered the people. Their instinct told them to flee. The opponent was closing in and they had no alternate solution but to choose flight. As danger lurked, people found desperate measures to escape. Some people hopped onto fishing boats, which was dangerous. The choppy waters of the ocean did not support Human Rights. Ironically, the ocean waters were just as dangerous as the army. Both had the brutal power to kill. The ocean cultivated a new form of fear. Danger lurked in the high waves. They were exposed to the angry nature of the choppy waves. The brutal force of the water rocked the fishing boats aggressively. The waves were unpredictable. If the boat capsized, they would all drown. Their chance of survival was challenged. The anticipation of danger had a devastating effect on women and children. They shook with fear and mental distress. The unknown temper of the sea caused panic attacks. They fiercely clung onto each other as huge waves rocked the boat. It was a dangerous voyage undertaken. Sometimes, the choppy waters intruded into the small fishing boat causing fear of drowning. A sense of survival was slim. The anticipation of danger caused tension and fear. They could not predict the problems, which would emerge. The ocean was not hospitable. The army could still shoot them.

Others attempted a more dangerous escape. They plotted to escape through the jungle. Large dangerous predators lurked in the jungle. The predators in the jungle were vibrant and animated. They undertook a journey of death. Wild animals lurked all around. Tigers, jaguars and elephants pose as a dangerous threat. Poisonous plants could cause their demise. The elephants were wild and angry in the jungle. Their temperament could not be predicted. Spiders, scorpions, ants and other dangerous insects made the jungle their natural habitat. They were not friendly hosts, but a foe to humans. Deadly serpents crawled around, slithering through the bush and trees. The jungle was infested with snakes. The cobra, constrictor snakes, pythons, and vipers blended in with the bushes and trees. Deadly snake bites were common in Sri Lanka. They were not equipped with the proper running shoes in the jungle. In the water-logged areas of the jungle, crocodiles were a source of fear. They made their way through the jungle during the day and at night. They faced mosquitoes, which could infect them with a deadly form of malaria.

The perception of walking through the jungle was dangerous. The potential of wild animals was reality. However, they had to take precaution against a more vicious, human foe. In the jungle, the army had the potential to capture and rape them. Life became defenceless. Several vines formed a net to trap them. They were not alert when they were physically exhausted. It was a dangerous game of hide and seek in the jungle. They were cautiously walking into the unknown. Ironically, they were risking their lives, in search for safety. Men, women and children undertook a dangerous excursion.

The humid conditions added to the challenge. There were no hospitals in the jungle to treat bites and infections. Tics, thorns and bugs were also an external source of conflict. Fear had limitations. They believed that the LTTE was fighting for them. They tried to escape from the LTTE area to the government areas. In the government area they were placed in IDP camps. Others joined extended family in Batticaloa and Trincomalee.

On a daily basis I communicated with the United Nations, Health Ministry and Red Cross to stop the war. I ordered food and medication from them. The Fishing Board helped me send people out, but I could not receive food.

On one notable day I was asleep. My sense of sound was evoked when I heard strange noises outside the hospital. The screams grew louder. It was gut wrenching screams. My stomach knotted. I felt intense fear. My instinct told me that danger lurked ahead. It was a cloudy day, which added to the gloom and the doom. People ran away from the beach towards the hospital, drenched in water. They were covered with sea sand like breaded chicken. Some were running with injured bodies. Others carried dead bodies in despair. The sea side was about 100 meters from the hospital.

People narrated the most dramatic and sensitive stories. Each had their own animated story. I listened with empathy to their sensitive stories of drowning. I felt as if I was listening to stories of the Titanic sinking.

The story about Kumaran's wife Ananthy and her baby brought me to tears. Ananthy was on the boat when it capsized. She held her baby close to her chest and clung to her. She fell off the boat with her baby, clinging on to her chest. This signified her demise. A fisherman was her cheerleader, motivating her to swim dramatically. She fought the ocean with all her might, clutching onto her baby for dear life. She tried to keep them afloat while swimming with one arm. The waves threw them around like a rag doll. The fisherman reached out to touch her but the waves manipulated the situation. They bobbed up and down as if on a trampoline. Her life became chaotic. It was difficult for her to swim, while clutching on to the baby. They dipped into the frigid waters and surfaced several times. The fisherman warned her of impending danger. His life was also in danger as the water formed a funnel around him.

"You cannot swim with the baby," he urged her to swim on.

"My baby," a mother's love was evident.

"Let go of the baby, then you can swim to safety," he negotiated with her.

"Not without my daughter," she cried as she plunged in.

"You need to swim with both hands. Let go of the baby," he pleaded.

"No no no," she cried in anguish.

"Let go, let go of the baby, you cannot save the baby. Let her go! Let her go," he tried to be logical.

"Nooooo no nono," the current was furious.

The fisherman was in danger because of the choppy waters. He had to leave her and save his own life. As danger loomed, she refused to let go of her baby. He watched as the malicious wave swallowed her and her baby.

Meantime others stood on shore watching dead bodies wash up on shore. Eventually Ananthy and her baby washed up on shore. Both had drowned. People cried hysterically to see a dead mother still clutching on to her dead baby. A mother's love never died. The heaven's gate opened up for both mother and baby. They were in the safe arms of the divine spirit.

At the hospital, I treated patients for drowning related illnesses. I sent ambulances and boats to the beach to save people. Earlier that day, Kumaran visited the hospital hoping to find his wife and baby. He looked at me with despair in his eyes. I could not break the news to him. He observed as dead bodies arrived at the hospital. Sadness filled the hospital corridors.

Kumaran and Ananthy were a young couple starting off a married life.

"Where is my wife?" he had some hope.

"She is gone," it was a difficult conversation.

"My baby?" anxiety took control of him.

"Gone," I was empathetic.

"Why did they leave me alone," he lost all self-control.

He was overwhelmed with grief. His hysterical cries echoed through the hallway. He fell onto the floor and curled up in fetal position. Grief paralyzed him.

He could not escape from his own grief. A father's heart ache was evident. Dead bodies arrived by the dozens. The fisherman who tried to save Ananthy narrated his story to Kumaran. When her body was found it was laying there face down. When they turned the body around they noticed her clutching onto the baby, tightly. She let the fisherman know that if her baby drowned, she would drown too. A mother's love lived on. Kumaran went back to war and dedicated his life to fighting for his people.

CHAPTER 12

Early Years- Rewind

Puthukkudiyiruppu, better known as PTK, in the Mullaitivu District of Sri Lanka, experienced heavy artillery shelling, from the military. My classmate's parents owned a stall in the market. At 5PM his mother walked 700 meters to her home, to cook. There was no transportation and telephone. The aerial bomb attack caused panic in the crowd. People scattered like rabbits in every direction. The detonation and fragmentation of the blast injured and killed many. My friend's father sustained a traumatic injury to his leg, which required amputation. He struggled with pain and was rushed to the hospital. The aftermath of the aerial bombing was devastating. Neighbours rushed to inform the mother of the father's fatalities. She was incapable of bearing such grief and rushed back to the market. While she rushed to her husband's side, there was a second aerial bombardment. If she remained at home, her life would have been saved. The bombing at the market was at a vast scale. Such aerial bombardment, with its capacity to destroy, was delivered to destroy Tamil civilians. The casualties were Tamil civilians on their routine market trips. The artillery and aerial attack were detonated, to inflict destruction of Tamil civilians. Upon impact the forceful projectiles and shrapnel killed thousands of civilians. A sea of body parts and body organs evoked the sense of sight. The explosion generated devastating injuries. The offensive attack killed my friend's mother upon impact. She felt the urge to save her husband yet lost her own life. The image of splattered body parts and blood created a shock wave.

In the meantime, the father was rushed with other casualties to PTK hospital. My friend rushed to the hospital to be at his father's side.

"Where is Amma?" the situation induced fear, in the son.

"She is safe at home," there was a sigh of relief.

"Are you going to be alright Appa?" tears streamed down his cheeks.

"Yes, I am just happy Amma is safe. I sent her home to cook. Thank God, I did. It saved her life," the father observed his detached leg.

"Yes, thank God, Amma is safe!" my friend shared his father's sense of relief.

Genocide was demoralizing on innocent Tamil civilians. The attacks were persistent as the world shut their eyes. The media camera lens zoomed away from the ethnic cleansing. It was a juxtaposition of "Hotel Ruwanada."

"Uncle did you see the newspaper?" a downhearted voice announced the news.

"What news?" my friend's father was still in pain.

"News?" my friend empathized with the injured patients.

"Here uncle," the man handed a list of names of the deceased to him, woefully.

"No nonononoooo!" my friend's father fell into a melancholic state.

"Oh my God," my friend was grief stricken.

"But Amma was at home cooking. How did she get killed? It does not make sense, non-sense," his father was inconsolable.

"Amma's name is on the list of the dead, these wretched bleep bleep!" my friend woefully wept.

"Sorry uncle, so sorry!" the man was crestfallen, as the heartbroken father and son shed massive tears of pain.

Their tears rained down in torrents. The whole hospital ward was flooded with tears, as the list of the deceased was passed around. The PTK Hospital turned into a funeral parlour. The tears flowed like the monsoon rain. I cried because I lost a precious friendship. My best friend quit school at the age of 15, which left me isolated and devastated. The situation was notoriously difficult for me to perceive. I worried about my own parents and their safety. There was a periodic change in my moods. When alone my tears were like a jet stream. When in public, my altruistic nature surfaced, and I dedicated my time to caring for the injured, at the ripe age of 15.

My mind rewind to my early years. I was a 16-year-old boy, left alone on the streets to fend for myself, in utter poverty. I had no bubble wrap to protect me. I had no helicopter parenting. I was a young boy, with a heart of gold and a mind set on educational goals.

I pondered on my educational studies, which was at an early age and images of a folk story surfaced. I recalled the literature taught to me by my wise teachers, the Masters of education. At the age of 16, the story resurfaced in real life. Therefore, they say that Literature is a catalyst that delves deep down into the core of reality, exposing the true nature of human beings.

Imagery of the folk tale flooded my mind. Kovalan and Kannagi were married under the same caste system. Kannagi loved Kovalan unconditionally.

Kovalan had an affair with Madhavi, a dancer. Kannagi gave Kovalan all her wealth to splurge on his girlfriend Madhavi. Kannagi gave Kovalan her ankle bracelet of rubies. Kovalan went bankrupted after splurging on his mistress. He approached the Pandya King, Nedunj Cheliyan l, in Madurai. He attempted to sell the anklet to him, with a hope of recovering his fortune. However, the king accused Kovalan of stealing his wife's anklet, and without a fair trial he beheaded him. Kannagi went on a rampant rage and broke open the ankle bracelet to prove that her anklet had rubies, while the Queen's anklet had pearls. Kannagi raged like a hurricane wind, in an attempt to shame the King. This injustice caused the King to commit suicide. Kannagi cast a curse upon the city of Madurai and set the city ablaze. She departed from India and landed in Sri Lanka. The Sri Lankans worshipped her as their Goddess. The Tamil Hindus referred to her as Kannaki. In honour of Goddess Kannaki, they built several Temples, and each year they worship the holy festival of Kannaki.

In September 1991, my friends and I attended the Kannaki festival. There was a Nanthikkadal Lagoon near Mullaitivu, visible to the military. Like an army of worshippers, Tamils adorned in the most elegant, embellished religious clothing. Hindu civilians marched to perform their religious acts of devotion. It was a sacred act of worship, known as a pooja, which brought worshippers together in peace and harmony. They were there to symbolize the good and dispel all evil. It was a Hindu cosmos of love, as the essence of existence. Worshipers marched with beautiful golden trays filled with offerings of fruit and flowers for deities. Men, women and children chanted Hindu mantras as they carried water, milk, fruits, flowers and incense for Gods and Goddesses. They were happy to march towards the temple and bow down at the alter to perform their Hindu religious rites. It was a sacred pilgrimage, where Tamil Hindus of all walks of life performed a spiritual purification, to receive glorious blessings from their deities. Devotees flooded the epic Kannaki Temple to receive blessings from their guardian Goddess, who is a legend for all Tamil women.

The Vattappalai Temple was in Mullaitivu. The Vattappalai Kannaki Pongal, was sacred to all Tamil Hindus. The LTTE was not present in the location. The Sri Lankan government was fully aware of the religious festival. They observed the men, women and children, walking to the temple for the pooja. The military fired at the crowd of Tamil worshipers. Pooja fruit, coconut, flowers, money, milk, water and other religious items, were scattered all over. Elegant silk saris were strewn all over. The dead and the injured laid side by side. It was a scene from a horror movie. There was an aerial bombardment, where a plane randomly bombed the civilians, making their pilgrimage to the temple. The army advanced and fired. I lived 1 km from the PTK hospital where people were transported. Like running a marathon, I ran to the hospital. At the age of 16 years old, I bandaged the injured as if I was a professional doctor. Doctors at the PTK hospital relocated patients to the Jaffna hospital. I volunteered my services to treat the severely injured.

We lived with no electricity and transportation. I walked 4 km to school. We lived in extreme poverty. My parents joined me from Trincomalee. We got a tiny house but lived below the poverty line with no safe water supply and sanitation facilities. The basic human needs were not met. My father who worked in agriculture, abused alcohol. He gave the family no emotional support. I had no extrinsic motivation to study. I intrinsically motivated myself to study. In extreme poverty I lit a lamp with coconut oil, to provide me with light to study. I sat with my books on a hard floor, burning the midnight oil studying. Before each exam I visited a school building, to study at the school tables. I slept on the school table and returned home in the morning. It was imperative that I studied, to my full potential. My inner authoritative voice commanded that I studied hard.

Unfortunately, my studies were disrupted by a security guard, who posed as an antagonist.

"You cannot study at this school at night," he retorted.

"I am only studying sir," I pleaded.

"Do not come back to this school," he snapped.

"I want to study, please." My words were like a melody.

"If goods are stolen from this school, I will blame you... heard me," he retaliated.

"Yes sir," I acknowledged his command.

I felt like Oliver Twist bargaining for food, yet in my case I was bargaining for a study place. I search around and came across an open tutorial school to study at night. There was no security guard there. I studied like a bookworm. I passed my high school grades with flying colours. Poverty did not place a shackle around me. I did not let poverty ruin my grades and education. I was a diligent and conscientious student, who industriously studied to exceed expectations at school. In between studying, I earnestly worked with tenacity at minor jobs, to earn money to put my siblings and I through school.

Only 2% of students with the highest grades were chosen for Medical School. Two hundred students sat in for the Medical School entry level exams. However, only the top academic students were chosen for medical school. I religiously studied between eight to ten years at medical school, still living in poverty.

I engaged in my own business to put myself through medical school. At that stage war continued to rage havoc in Sri Lanka. The government banned camphor, batteries, noodles, nails and other items they believed would be used by the LTTE, to construct bombs. At the age of 16 years old and when I entered medical school, I purchased these banned items. I travelled from place to place by bicycle, day and night under dangerous circumstances. I hid the banned items in my clothing. At home I sold the items for a profit to make money for my studies. I even rode my bicycle to purchase carousel oil. I carried 100 litres by bicycle to sell. I was weak. I fell off my bike several times. However, I found the strength and power to continue.

My spiritual guardian angels had to be present, prompting me along with all my endeavours. The universe undertook to support and protect me, through my life-threatening ventures. I rode my bicycle with no light at night. Sometimes, the aerial bombing provided me with light, to illuminate my path. It is ironical, how something so negative, would provide me a positive illuminated path. Nevertheless, it provided me with money to support my studies at medical school. I continued to pass my exams at medical school, with high marks.

I undertook a risky mission to accomplish business. I used a fishing boat to transport carousel. If I acquired more money, I paid a truck to transport me across the dangerous lagoon, for the sake of business. If I did not have money I rode my bicycle. I risked my life because the Navy could fire at me. From Kilinochchi to Jaffna a boat helped me. It was dangerous, but I needed to do business for money, to put me through school and medical school. I lived life on a dangerous lane.

In today's society what I did from the age of 11 years old, is noted as child labour but for me it was a means of survival. During my escapade of transporting carousel oil in barrels, my skin peeled off my hand like paint peeling off a wall. It was the price I paid to save money for the sake of education. Vehicles needed carousel oil to move since they could not afford gas.

I was in Medical school when the Navaali Church was bombed, in 1995. The 20-year-old ancient church housed those who believed that God would help them if they took refuge in a church. The military always bombed crowded areas. The beautiful church became a ruin when it was bombed by the military. Casualties were rushed to hospital on motor bikes. As a medical student, I lent a helping hand to treat the injured. Chandrika Bandaranaike the president at that time lost her husband during the war. Tamils supported her because she was symbolic of the "peace dove". We expected more from her, but she banned needed items. The massacre increased during her reign.

Blood was required for transfusions. I voluntarily donated blood every six months to aid the injured at the hospitals. I helped remove the dead bodies at the hospital. I was spiritually strong. I collected clothing from people and distributed it amongst those displaced during the war. I volunteered to help out with administration in the hospital. People feared the military because they raped and killed women.

In 1997, twenty students were selected from the all Tamil Mullaitivu District. We had to follow the protocol of military clearance and approval. We were transported from Trincomalee to Jaffna via a large boat. Students suffered severe motion sickness. Our sense of balance and equilibrium was altered. Nausea was the common symptom. Vomit dominated our sense of smell. The ailment of diarrhea dominated the sea voyage. It was as if it was contagious, yet not. The waters were choppy and threw us around like rag dolls. I focused on my breathing and closed my eyes and slept.

When the chosen medical students arrived in Jaffna we were searched at military checkpoints every 200 meters. The military checked out bodies and bags. There was no sophisticated body checking with females. Female body checking, by the military encompassed intimate touching and seduction, which was morally and ethically wrong. Female fundamental rights were violated by the military. The military officers were unrefined and giggled in a crude manner, as they intimately touched the females, with a sexual connotation. They provoked their own sexual arousal, with the notion of vulgar touching. They treated females as sexual ornaments.

Medical students were issued a new ID card and University ID. Our National ID became invalid in Jaffna. Attending University during the war was challenging. Due to the war and displacement, numerous houses were abandoned in Jaffna. University students used the abandoned homes as residence. There was a sign on the door stating *University Student Hostel.* If the residents returned, we had to vacate the premises. Alternately, we paid the owners a little rent. We kept their houses clean and safe. We had a curfew. We feared the army due to their history of violence and rape.

A famous rape case was one of an eighteen-year-old student. The military kidnapped her and raped her over two days. They gang raped and tortured her. The army scouted around for young families. The military officials raped the women, while violently beating up her husband. The military officials also stalked young women and watched them taking a shower or bath.

Those chilling incidents were common. The military officers were not incarcerated. If people reported the incident, they were brutally killed. They stalked women and young girls with an intention to rape them. These incidents were a human right issue, yet it escalated. They displayed power over women and were sexual perpetrators.

The 18-year-old's relative who was a lawyer filed a case against the military. The case took a year to get to court. My wife's friend walked home alone when she was violently raped by military officials in an abandoned home. Her family searched for her. They heard screams but thought nothing of it. The military evoked fear in women. The military officials strategically buried her body in a toilet pit. The owner returned to his abandoned home a year later. When cleaning the sanitary-pit he found her body. The ramifications were devastating. The military had no capacity of empathy. They displayed apathy to women and their families. Rape clarified their status of being dominant males. Justice was not brought to the violent perpetrators. The unbridled violence was infinite. Rape was premediated by the military officers.

I completed medical school in 2004 and opted to study for my master's degree as a pediatrician. War shattered and destroyed families. I did not allow the war to shatter my integrity and confidence to help the injured. The military check points became a challenge. People had to sleep at the border points overnight and cross over in the morning. At night the military officials raped women and set them free. The women were paranoid with fear and did not report the case.

The incident angered the LTTE. They frowned at seeing Tamil women being raped. The LTTE moved their check points close to the military to solve the problem of rape. The LTTE encouraged women and children to stay at the LTTE check points overnight. In 1993, a police station and court were established in the vicinity.

CHAPTER 13

Artillery Attacks

When the PTK hospital was finally attacked by the military doctors, nurses and patients moved to Puthumaththalan Hospital. It was like a domino effect moving from one hospital to the next. It became a chain reaction like dominos falling down, due to the military artillery attacks on the hospitals.

The PTK hospital had a Temple and a Church beside each other. Patients and their families slept in the Ganesha temple and the Church believing that God is their saviour and he would protect them. They cherished their belief in Lord Ganesha and Jesus and encompassed their protection in their heads. The military imposed a final artillery attack on the PTK hospital. Ganesha emerged as a power to remove obstacles. He bestowed upon patron's wisdom and intellect. I walked into the temple at the ruined hospital to see the supreme deity beheaded. Lord Ganesha's body parts were shattered all over the temple, mingled with dead bodies and human body parts. Ironically, God could not save himself or his devotees. I proceeded to the Church and was appalled to see the statue of Jesus exploded, with the parts scattered over dead bodies. Death loomed over them. He did not save them, yet he accompanied his patrons to heaven, a place of peace and harmony. The bells from the temple and church tolled in jubilation for the souls departing to a peaceful land.

We moved to the Puthumaththalan hospital with medication and equipment from PTK hospital. I donated money to purchase tents and equipment for the makeshift wards. People slept under mango and coconut trees. They cooked food outside, despite the danger of insects and snakes.

The major problem was there were no toilets. People constructed makeshift lavatory facilities out of wood. People lined up to go to the toilets as if lining up for tickets to a rock concert. There were about two hundred people patiently waiting for one toilet. Each person waiting had one litre of water, in a coke bottle to flush the makeshift toilet. It always plugged after two days. I had to send maintenance workers to fix the problem. On one particular day, I observed a young girl about 20 years old, waiting to use the latrine. The urgency to defecate was severe. She could not control her urge to urinate and pass stools. Diarrhea dripped down her legs, as she waited for the toilet pit. The watery stools made its way down her legs like a tributary. The lower part of her body was contaminated with loose running stools. I wondered what she had consumed. She lost control over her bowel movements. There were about a thousand people in line to use the toilet pit. Other people went to the paddy fields at night to defecate. Others dug sand pits in between their shelters to use as sanitary facilities. Others emptied their bowels in the beach water. When nature called there was an urgency to go. The waves rolled in with feces. Excrement was all over. Human beings had to resort to animal tactics to discharge feces. The water and toilet crisis were chronic. Others who tried to bath in the beach water were faced with feces due to defecation. At times the temporary toilets collapse due to the seasonal topical rains. Artillery shelling also released the feces from the ground.

Some people slept in bunkers made of sand to protect themselves from the military. It was a fortification to protect themselves from the artillery attacks. The bunkers were sand trenches dug out in the ground. However, when they were bombarded with aerial attacks, the sand bunkers, which were once homes to Tamil civilians, became graves after the military attacks. The explosions caused internal ear injuries to others.

I could not sleep because of the sound of the continuous shelling. The doctors rotated with their scheduled sleep times. I did not want to sleep in the sand bunker trenches because of the lack of oxygen. I slept outside, on the beach sand, under the Palmyra Tree. The Palmyra tree became my shelter and my bedroom. With beach sand, I made a makeshift pillow. I covered my sand pillow with my saaram or lungi, better known as a sarong in the western culture. I tied another saaram tightly around my head and ears like a bandage, to filter out the noise from the military bombs and shelling. I used the Palmyra fruit to wash my clothing, as the other civilians did. There was no soap. The Palmyra fruit was used as soap. Unfortunately, the cows included the Palmyra fruit in their diet. Therefore, when the people hung their clothing to dry, the smell of the Palmyra fruit attracted the cows and they ate the clothing. I used another saaram or sarong as a blanket. I was subject to shelling, snake bites and insect bites. It became dangerous sleeping in loose sea sand, outside.

The Red Cross members slept at the church. They were guests of the priest and nuns. Later I was invited to stay at the church with Dr. Thangamuttu Sathyamurthi. We could not sleep at the hospital because of continuous hysterical crying. Crying became animated. It was histrionic crying that filled the wards of the hospital day and night. Crying became contagious. People cried watching others cry uncontrollably. I could not keep a stone face watching them cry. Crying was like a relay sport.

The church was one mile from the hospital. My mother was nearby, so she cooked for me and did my laundry. The Tamil Rehabilitation Organization TRO delivered food to the patients, such as dhal, rice, curry and dried fish. However, due to the shortage of supplies the dhal was weak and watery as soup.

People did not have money because they feared working during the war. The army stole money from businessmen. The Diaspora from Canada, U.S.A and France sent money to help relatives. I asked businessmen to help the people obtain money.

Hundreds of casualties arrived at the hospital daily. I arranged mobile and outpatient clinics to serve patients injured by the military. The road was guttered and blocked. I negotiated with the Red Cross to inform the government that ships were needed to transport patient and their close nuclear families to Trincomalee. The Red Cross ships anchored about 3km from the beach. Fishing boats transported patients, through choppy waters to the ship. After surgery patients were shipped out to the ship. About 300 patients left weekly. The military called cease fire, while patients were transported by the Red Cross. When the Red Cross left, the military aggressively fired, and more patients registered at the hospital. I dealt with the worst cases of amputations and stomach injuries. I had to cut down on the use of anaesthesia because of the shortage.

The Sri Lankan government placed a ban on foreign doctors, journalist and organizations from entering the war zone. Eventually the Indian government sent doctors to the war zone hospitals, close to Mullaitivu. The Red Cross delivered a small amount of medication for war related injuries. The government blatantly refused to send blood and anaesthesia.

Fortunately, the LTTE provided us with medication. Since saline was limited, I improvised by using water from the King Coconut. It was sterile and healthy. To our dismay the coconut tree was bombarded by the military, which made it scarce. Tamil civilians, who went to pluck coconuts off the palm trees, were shelled. The army fired at hungry people in search of food.

I further improvised by using the leaves from the Palmyra trees for medical purposes. We did not have any plaster of Paris to construct casts, which was needed to immobilize fractured bones. I spontaneously used parts of the Palmyra plant as a makeshift plaster of Paris. The government was afraid that the LTTE would use the plaster of Paris to produce weapons. We had to engage in impromptu methods to solve problems. Surgical bandage and gauze were not available. I visited a nearby textile store and purchased cotton saris to use as bandages. After an operation I cleaned the stomach with the improvised sari bandages. A small businessman, who ran a grocery store, had a haberdashery section. I sterilized all items by boiling them. I purchased several items, which I stored in my car. If the hospital was bombed, then I had items for the people.

I was friendly with all the people around, especially those who ran business in the areas. As I passed their stores they waved at me. However, it was like an eerie interlude. I felt as if I had taken a ghost path because when I returned the stores were not there. Artillery shells fell upon the stores, killing the people and destroying the buildings. I felt like an alien creature in a valley of ashes, surrounded by the fire of hell. The military had crippled the area with mutilated body parts, in a setting envisioned as hell. I rolled up my car windows. I blasted my music, to muffle the sound of the military gun shots and shelling. I sped through the roads like a concord, with supersonic power. I tried not to think too much. I erased my inner dialogue with myself. It was my psychological therapy. My fast driving helped me dodge the bullets. When I took a driver with me, I used a cutting board as a shield against the window. There were no cars or people on the roads. I was not afraid of death. I was a cat with nine lives.

I contacted pneumonia, accompanied by a high fever. Another Doctor was my senior, who was five years older than me. We worked hand in hand, on the same wavelength. We got along well and were in sync with all that we did for the hospital. We sang the same song of conflict in the war zone. We were the last remaining doctors, with three others in the war zone. We worked in good taste. We extrinsically motivated each other to support our patients. I gained knowledge from his experience. I was close to death with pneumonia, yet I continued to work, as my voice took a leave of absence. Together with other doctors we built hospitals in Mullivaikal and Valavharmadam.

On April 19, 2009, the shelling was continuous and furious. We could not sleep because of the intense noise. Another Doctor slept in the trench while I bandaged my head with my saaram to filter the sound and slept on the bed. Another doctor informed us that the military was drawing close, like a lion stalking its prey. The doctors stole my car keys because they did not want me to drive to the hospital close to the military, out of fear of losing me. The military and the LTTE were on either side. Some people ran to the military, whereas others felt safe with the LTTE. It was pandemonium. We were upset that some doctors went to the army-controlled area, with no return.

I begged for my vehicle keys. I drove along the shoreline and headed in the direction of the military. Ding, ding, ding, ding, and ding bullets bounced off my vehicle. The military feared that vehicles were driven by the Black Tigers, with chemical weapons. I noticed the military. I ran to the Palmyra tree for cover. I heard histrionic cries. I peered from the side of the tree bark and my eyes froze. Dead bodies were shattered all around. I ducked and dived and crawled like a stalking lion to the hospital. The hospital building was destroyed. The Tamils feared the military. I grabbed items and some patients and headed to Mullivaikal. It was the worst time of my life, as the shelling persisted to the maximum. There was a cloud on the horizon as the fates of Tamils were worse than death. It was a rough ride to hell.

"Your mom came to the hospital to check on you," an employee notified me.

"That's a mother's love," another patient validated.

"What was funny is that she ran all the way wearing a motorbike helmet, to protect her head against shelling," a patient giggled.

"I told her that you were not here," my friend explained.

"I know she is so worried about me," I cried.

It was torrid times. The Tamil community had a rough ride. We were in a tight corner with the dilemma of war. A LTTE sector member asked me to crawl to the beach where he would pick me up with an ambulance. I was on the horns of a dilemma. I struggled between saving myself and saving my patients. He turned on the ambulance siren and met me at the beach. I ran like a rodent afraid of humans.

I treated everyone fairly and sensibly. I had reasonable judgement and did not favour one over the next. One day I went home for lunch and my mother was not there.

"Where is amma?" I was curious.

"Some place is giving out sugar. She went to get some sugar," my sister acknowledged.

"She is standing in a line for eight hours just for 250g sugar," my sister continued.

I had 150 kilos sugar, milk powder and dhal at the hospital. I was honest. It was for my patients. I did not want to distribute it amongst family, relatives, or friends. I rode the moral horse. Honesty was important to me. I could not discriminate in times of war. I could not be bias. My parents were 65 and 68 years old at that time. Relatives and friends whom I did not help out with food stopped talking to me. It was a fair game, during unfair times.

The military captured 100 000 people on April 20, 2009 in the No Fire Zone. The BBC questioned the army.

"I see you have 50 000 people I say," the BBC journalist acknowledged.

"Yes," a military official confirmed.

"But earlier on you released a statement confirming that you had 100 000 Tamils, indeed!" the journalist was baffled.

"Oh! you remember," the military officer laughed like a hag.

"So why are you not truthful," the BBC journalist frowned.

"Oh!" was all he could say.

That was the modus operandi of the military. They killed thousands of Tamils yet denied killing them. They did not account for the ones they killed.

Mullivaikal west had outdoor hospitals under tamarind trees. Patients slept outside, as if it was fully air conditioned. When it rained they slept in the rain, which was like a bathroom shower. They had no option. Unfortunately, patients were in the rain for days. After surgery a tent was rolled out on the paddy, field for them to sleep on. The military destroyed the hospitals.

We moved to Mullivaikal east, into a small primary school. We crawled around like cats as the gun fire increased. They fired from one junction to the next, which was etched in my memory. Sometimes we slithered on our tummies like snakes, to avoid the bullets. Bullets spread past me like a gust of wind. Suddenly, an artillery shell fell about kilo close to me. The sand smelled like smoke. Sand sprayed me like a garden hose. This genocide cannot fall on deaf ears.

"Doctor come, run run!" a voice completed with the shelling at a loud tone.

"I am dusting myself," I laughed while dusting off the sand.

"You are laughing," the voice cried.

"I am not afraid of death," I continued to dust myself off.

There were two hospitals on the West and East in Mullivaikal. A female doctor was killed in the west.

A LTTE doctor was killed. The pain was etched in my heart as I recalled the incident.

"Doctor can I borrow your stethoscope," a young doctor requested.

"Yes, I bought this stethoscope 3 years ago. It is one of the best," I gloated with pride.

"I know it is expensive," she smiled.

She helped to monitor my patients, while I went out for lunch. When I returned the hospital was shelled and she was killed. My stethoscope was shattered as her body parts were scattered.

Mullivaikal was divided into parts of East and West. The Tamil caste system existed. People in the east and west were divided into Vellalar caste, which were agricultural society. The Karaiyar caste found on the eastern coastal areas were the fishing society. Then people referred to the east and west as the Vellalar and the Karaiya. It then became known as the east and the west.

I proceeded to Mullivaikal east. We were surrounded by shelling, with numerous deaths. Families left the dead relatives at the hospital for us bury. There were no people to identify dead bodies. There was no time. Time flew by as fast as the bullets. People could be identified by only clothing due to the decomposing bodies. I helped bury the dead as the nightmare continued. I had the task of collecting dead bodies for burial. Each day another one bites the dust. I had several brushes with death. I cheated death several times, as I was at death's door. I was a dead man walking! I diced with death.

CHAPTER 14

The Great Escape

After my release, the government refused to give me a director position, as a doctor in the hospital. It amounted to inside politics. I knew that power was in the hands of the government. Changes depended on the authority and did not work to my benefit. My status was lowered, and I did not receive any personal gains. They did not pay me for overtime and extra salary in the war zone. Organizational policies had a destructive impact on me. The political landscape after the war was unstable and imbalanced. I worked at the hospital as a normal doctor. Those who engaged in such policies did it for personal gains.

The war had a drastic impact on me physically. The injuries, which I sustained, had an impact on my work life. When I was injured due to the bombing, my right hand was paralysed. It was a complex situation, since I could not use my right hand. The notion of not using my right hand did not dampen my spirits. Since my dominant hand could not be used, I taught myself to use my left hand. My brain worked overtime to create a new neural link. It was a challenge, but I was ready to conquer any challenge that confronted me. I had been through the worst and the best was yet to come. I had to become ambidextrous. I put patience into practise. I became proficient at using my left hand, with daily practice. Frustration tried to cripple me. I did not give into frustration. I had to develop my fine and gross motor skills like a kindergarten child. My left-hand muscles had to be trained. I made a conscious effort to make a significant difference. Patients often laugh at the way doctors write prescriptions. Their writing is illegible. I gained neatness and accuracy by using my left hand. I intrinsically motivated myself to practise. Like a child, I traced over dotted lines. I was a doctor who became a teacher, teaching myself how to write and eat with my left hand. I was highly successful. I exceeded expectations in training my left hand.

The Tamil Diaspora were Tamil immigrants. They emigrated from Sri Lanka, worldwide. Those of Tamil descent emigrated to Canada, London, Malaysia, South Africa, Singapore, Mauritius, and throughout Europe. They formed a global population worldwide. After the war, Sri Lankan Tamils dispersed like wild mustard seeds around the world. A large number of

Tamils entered countries as refugees. South Africa, Canada, United Kingdom, India, Australia, the United States, Seychelles, and Europe took in many Tamil refugees.

The Tamil Diaspora politics began to surface. The Diaspora organizations worldwide collected funds to send back to Sri Lanka to rebuild the Tamil areas destroyed during the war. The Tamil Diaspora played an integral role in collecting funds worldwide. Although, they were stationed in different countries, they played an active role in contributing towards the Tamil sectors in Sri Lanka. The Tamil expatriates formed the Tamil Diaspora. They also played a vital role in appealing to the leaders of their host countries, to put an end to the Tamil genocide in Sri Lanka. They took their positions on the international sphere. They lobbied together on the international stage. They advocated for peace in Sri Lanka. They implemented measures to embrace the rights and freedom of all Tamils in Sri Lanka. They preserve the Tamil rights, and culture ahead. Maaveerar Naal, better known as the Great Heroes Day, is a day which Tamils dedicate to their martyrs. It is equivalent to Remembrance Day. Their ideology is geared towards safeguarding the Tamil culture.

The Tamil Diaspora extended their helping hand, as they promised to pay for the needs of the patients. Money was funded and collected overseas. They did not keep up to their promise. The Tamil Diaspora from London and Canada negotiated to pay for the patients' needs. I purchased blankets, bed sheets, linen and tarps for the hospital. It cost $30,000. I paid out of my own pocket, with the notion of collecting the money from the Tamil Diaspora abroad. I extended the shelters and documented the progress. The superiors did not acknowledge the $500,000 rupees spent. Unfortunately, corruption and bribing set in, when the Tamil Diaspora pocketed the money, for their own financial gain. I invested money in the building structures yet was not compensated for the effect.

The Tamils displaced during the war needed charity. The Tamil Diaspora was not transparent in spending of charitable funds. Tamilians, orphans, the handicap, single parents, injured and displaced families, were in need of financial help. The C.I.D followed me.

"Sir, the commander needs to see you," a C.I.D officer was blunt.

"Are you from the military group?" I was not naive.

"We need money," the words rolled out of his mouth like musical notes.

"Your commander can meet me in the hospital," I invited him to a safe zone.

"We know where your siblings and parents live," I took that as a threat.

"The government can arrest you at any time," his words were intimidating, like a dagger in my back,

"Why are you doing this to me? The C.I.D did not give me back my job," my words rolled out like golf balls.

Once again, my life was in sheer danger. I knew that Switzerland and U.S.A accepted refugees. I knew that I had to seek asylum in a safe country. With the help of a friend, I played an instrumental role to safeguard my family. The Swiss Embassy advised me to visit the U.S.A embassy because of the language barrier. The Swiss embassy sensed the danger and contacted the U.S.A embassy.

The situation was tense and highly secretive. I undertook a dangerous mission. It was a mission impossible. I needed international protection. Our conversations were through emails. I needed to be assessed. I received a U.S.A identification and I met a U.S.A immigration affair in Colombo. My heart was in my mouth and I was nervous. The last time I was in Colombo, I was on the 4th floor. My hair stood at ends, as I undertook my journey to Colombo.

I was so nervous that I was afraid of my own shadow. The C.I.D made my blood run cold. I was in shock and scared. The Swiss and U.S.A officials worked hand in hand, and they appointed a lawyer to help me. The lawyer and I met weekly. I had a bundle of nerves. I was tense and worried about being caught. I narrated my story to the lawyer, who listened attentively. It took three weeks to finish the asylum application. Needless to say, the U.S.A embassy was friendly and helpful. I was like a cat on hot bricks, because I was restless and afraid of being caught. The Human Rights Organization paid for my lawyer and meeting room. The documents were submitted, and the waiting period was three months. During that period, I was on the edge of my seat. I was nervous of being caught. I had to have eyes at the back of my head. I walked around as if I had a siren on my head.

I lived in fear in Sri Lanka. If the Sri Lankan government discovered my ulterior motives, I would have been arrested and tortured again. I did not want to get my fingers burnt and suffer the results. My heart missed a beat each time I saw a white van. The white van was notoriously known for capturing Tamils suspected of going against the will of the government. I held my breath, while waiting for my papers. I was always anxious.

I escaped with my wife and my child to Nepal. The Sri Lankan newspapers spread rumours about me. The newspaper article read:

THE DOCTOR ESCAPED

The government official (staff reporter)

"Dr. Varatharajah Thurairajah found in Nepal"

2009 - The Tamil Diaspora in Nepal, South Asia, (located in the Himalayas) helped Dr. Varatharajah Thurairajah escape. However, it is believed that from Nepal, he escaped to England. The Sri Lankan government has been alerted about his whereabouts. The Sri Lankan military and the C.I.D department are on the alert in search of him. It is believed that he escaped Sri Lanka about 3 weeks ago.

Dr. Varatharajah Thurairajah's work at the hospital will be terminated. He is given a forced vacation for now.

According to a military officer, "Dr. Varatharajah Thurairajah told me that he was going to India for medical treatment."

We were going to give him forced vacation from the hospital for three months. However, we decided to give him forced vacation after a month."

A government official commented, "He accidently injured his right arm during the war. He needs medical attention."

The Sri Lankan government is still in search of Dr. Varatharajah Thurairajah's place of stay. He will be brought back to Sri Lanka, when our military officers find him.

Other military officials suspect that he has left India, and escaped to England, with the help of the Diaspora. The matter is being looked into.

A spokesman at the hospital noted, "Dr. Varatharajah Thurairajah left abruptly, with less notice."

It is the duty of Sri Lankan government and the military officers to see to it that Dr. Varatharajah

Thurairajah, resumes his position at the hospital soon."We also suspect that he is a member of the LTTE."

....

After the civil war ended the Sri Lankan government broke all Human Rights protocol. They continued to rape, kidnap, and torture innocent Tamil men, women and children. I knew that they would kill me if they found me in Nepal. I was scared out of my wits. I lost control of my confidence because I was so afraid. Each time, I spotted a white van in Nepal, it scared the living daylights out of me. Darkness surrounded me, and my inner light switched off.

The International Organization of Migration protected me like a mother protecting her child. They changed my hotel every week. My attitude of gratitude was extended to them because they also paid for my hotel room. I batten down the hatches. I always remembered to close and lock the doors behind me. I was afraid that the C.I.D would find me or follow me. The (UNHCR), UN Refugee Agency, secretly picked me up from the airport. My case was a challenge to them. If found the Sri Lankan government would have killed me.

"You are now with us but still not safe Doctor," A Nepal U.S.A embassy official declared.

"I am so afraid," I shook as if I had a fit of epilepsy.

"We will take you to a hotel. However, you have to rotate cities and hotels," he affirmed.

"Thank you so much. I will do everything in my power to stay safe," the situation was dicey and unpredictable.

Since my life was fraught with danger, I could not predict if I was going to die. Fear followed me around like a shadow.

The unexpected became the expected. I continued to worry about being abducted by the Sri Lankan government. The statistics of abduction was high. It was no hoax that thousands of Tamils were abducted, and their trails were diminished. The Human Rights organizations ensured my safety. I continued to remain safety conscious. I could not let anyone manipulate my safety. That uneasy feeling gave me butterflies in my stomach. It took a lot of energy to mentally rehearse self-protection. I yanked myself away from anyone who entered my personal bubble. I became paranoid. Paranoia was necessary to protect myself from any conspiracy, from the Sri Lankan government. It was not a matter of delusion, but it involved inner instinct of perceiving danger. I scrutinized everyone around me. My dysphonic self-consciousness was evident.

On one particular day at about 7pm, danger lurked around me. My wife, daughter and I were on the 10th floor of a hotel. My wife engaged in a conversation with a relative on Skype, while my child lay next to her on the bed. The shift was swift and unexpected. Panic was the dominant sensation. I hit the panic button and my body reacted with fear and confusion.

I was quaking in my boots. As I shook the room shook with me, as if experiencing the same panic attack. I was skating on thin ice, in the risky situation. I thought about the shelling during the war. This was a juxtaposition of the same situation.

"What's going on?" my wife was terrified.

"Do you hear that?" my wife's senses were alerted.

"Gut wrenching screams!" it evoked my sense of sound.

"Look everyone's outside," my wife drew the curtains.

"Come let's go too… our baby!" it was flight not fight.

I ran away from calamity. The war zone was a catastrophe. I found myself in a stroke of bad luck, when earthquake hit Nepal. It was a magnitude of 8 on the Richter scale. The earthquake triggered fear in people. Thousands of Nepalese were homeless. About ten thousand people died. About twenty-five people were injured. The damage was estimated in billions. It was as if the Universe tested my strength and courage. The aftershocks were devastating.

High rise buildings in the capital Kathmandu toppled down, like an implosion. Other buildings came down like an avalanche. I faced the challenge of an 8.1 magnitude earthquake. Two worst disasters fell upon me. My life came to a total standstill. Sri Lanka needed rebuilding after the fatal war. Nepal needed rebuilding after the devastating earthquake. I had to rebuild and reconstruct my own life. The paralysis of my own body, physically, socially and psychologically needed attention. The Human Rights organization called to check on my safety. I laughed nervously because I escaped the war zone and fell into an earthquake zone. I wondered what message the Universe had for me.

I had a brush with death several times. I came so close to death in the war zone and with the Nepal earthquake. I really cheated death. In both cases I narrowly avoided death. I was a dead man walking. My life was surrounded by great danger. The earthquake and the war were a painful demise. I accumulated all the bad incidents that were thrown upon me. It was the death of a thousand cuts. In both situations, death surrounded me. Death taught me about danger. I was forced to dice with death. I was surrounded by danger. I was not going to give in to death. I was a fighter. Death was not going to transport me from the cradle to the grave. My life's purpose on earth was not complete. The universe had a better plan for me.

Each struggle, which I encountered, made me a stronger person. Conflict built my character traits. The more struggles I encountered, the stronger it made me. My spiritual growth was evident. It was all a ghost of a chance. With every fall I succeeded. It was hope that delivered strength to me. The universe placed the virtue of trust in me. It placed new values in my life. I was not ready to meet my maker. It was not time to die. Spiritually I became a strong soul, ready to bring justice in this world of turmoil and hate. The skeleton in the closet needed to be exposed. The deep, dark, dangerous and deadly secrets of the government army need to be exposed.

My attitude of gratitude is extended to those members of the Human Rights groups who transported me and my nuclear family from Nepal to Hong Kong, to New York and finally to Louisville Kentucky, U.S.A. The case worker picked us up from the airport. They paid for our rent, food, clothes and other needs for six-months. They helped me for the next five years.

I worried about the extended family I left behind in Sri Lanka. I arrived in U.S.A on November 15, 2011. I did not tell any extended family about my departure because it was the great escape. It had to be kept as a top secret for the personal safety of me and my nuclear family. I was like a thief in the night. All my plans were secretive. My lips were sealed. Even my parents did not know about my plans and actions. It was difficult to keep a poker face, while plotting my escape. I had to cover my tracks. I could not leave any evidence. I had to conceal my movements. I kept a low profile, while on the run. I could not attract any attention. It was sad to keep my parents in the dark. I could not reveal any information for I was afraid of any whistle blower. The government had informants all over. My wife and child's safety were also crucial to me. The news evoked fear in me. Adjustment in a new country was difficult. Not having a job created fear and frustration in me.

I had to go back to medical school in U.S.A. From a prominent doctor, I became a medical student. Friends helped me through the initial period. I participated in several United Nations human rights meetings, in South Africa and Canada. Participation with the Diaspora was crucial. Funds had to be raised for the war zones in Sri Lanka, where Tamil civilians were displaced. Eventually, I received my medical license in U.S.A. Then, I had to apply for the residential programme. Who said life was easy?

After all these years, my mind reflects on my five senses. Images of my past flashed in my present. I take a walk down memory lane evoking all of my five senses and multiple expressions.

War was not a pleasant sight,

Killing people was just not right,

In the blink of an eye,

I watched Tamil people die,

I was the apple of their eye,

What the army revealed was a lie,

No, I will not turn a blind eye,

Viewing dead bodies made me cry,

Yes, it evoked a sense of sight,

It was a bloody, vicious fight.

It also evoked my sense of smell,

On the smell of blood I dwell,

Imagine, to follow your nose,

Instincts said that the army was close,

Definitely I did smell a rat,

My hospital bed was only a mat,

For safety I had to sniff around,

To investigate the shelling sound,

And I had to turn my nose up,

Smell of tea from a dirty cup,

My injuries under the officer's nose,

I needed medication by the dose,

Yes, it evoked a sense of smell,

It is a story that I have to tell.

It evoked a sense of hearing,

As the government army was nearing,

Have to say my ears were burning,

The sound of shelling was churning,

Army had nothing between the ears,

The brutal cries were sounds of fears,

In a situation that was out on your ear,

Disgraced and free, I shed a tear,

An even to bend someone's ear,

The army pestered me when they were near,

And to keep my ear to the ground,

Genocide is what I heard all around,

As a doctor I had to be caring.

And to evoke the sense of taste,

This genocide was such a waste,

It left a bad taste in my mouth,

With disgust I had no doubt,

For saliva we acquired a taste,

Food was delivered with no haste,

And genocide was in poor taste,

Dried blood formed a nasty paste,

They need a taste of their own medicine,

Killing Tamil civilians is an evil sin,

The government had to taste blood,

Dead bodies arrived like a flood,

Definitely evokes a sense of taste,

Genocide is an act of distaste.

And it evoked my sense of touch,

The act of genocide was way too much,

I am in a safe country, touch wood,

Massive killing in every neighbourhood,

The government army hit a nerve,

To be put on trial is what they deserve,

With my patients I keep in touch,

To those dreadful memories I clutch,

With human rights I touch base,

Genocide is a human rights case,

For me it was a case of touch and go,

 Had to run away from the foe,

It evoked my sense of touch,

My country of birth I miss so much!

Genre: Memoir

Dr. Varatharajah Thurairajah

Dr. Varatharajah Thurairajah was born on March 3rd, 1975. He is also known as Dr. Varathan. He was born in a small village in Thampalagamam, in the Trincomalee District, in Sri Lanka. It is a rural district famous for the paddy fields, rice, banana and coconut plantations. The Koneswaram Temple and the Kanthali water tank are important to the history of the District. His transition from childhood to adulthood was complex, as he experienced child poverty, child labour, social injustices, cultural cleansing, economic deprivation, physical and emotional vulnerability. Government policies and cultural discrimination contributed significantly to poverty. As a child he was traumatized by war and given no fundamental rights, during the armed conflict between the Sri Lankan Government and the LTTE. The army targeted schools and homes forcing him to leave school at the age of eleven. Varatharajah worked as a "coolie" in the paddy fields for minimum wage. The money earned was used for school supplies. When the army invaded his village he escaped with his parents to Kinniya, a Muslim area. As a child, he engaged in treating war casualties, which intrinsically motivated him to become a doctor. He also worked at a grocery store packing food, to save money for his education. His family was poverty stricken. At the vulnerable age of 15, he experienced disturbing human suffering. Boys his age were necklaced with vehicle tires and set on fire, by the military. He undertook a dangerous journey to escape through the jungles and murky rivers. He sustained injuries through insect bites, thorns and crab bites. He almost lost his life through indiscriminate firing by the Navy and the military. Poverty introduced him to the gnawing feelings of hunger pangs. Despite living in extreme poverty, he visualized his educational goals. With no electricity, he studied with candlelight, which did not deter him to exceed expectations in all his educational goals. He aspired to succeed at school. By working around the clock, with work and school, he excelled in his external examinations and was one of the few people who were accepted to Medical School. Finally, he graduated as a successful doctor who treated patients in the war zone.

36721650R00142

Made in the USA
Lexington, KY
17 April 2019